The
Melting Pot
and the Altar

The John K. Fesler Memorial Fund provided assistance in the publication of this volume, for which the University of Minnesota Press is grateful.

The Melting Pot and the Altar

Marital Assimilation in Early Twentieth-Century Wisconsin

Richard M. Bernard

Assistant Professor of History, Marquette University

UNIVERSITY OF MINNESOTA PRESS □ MINNEAPOLIS

Published by the University of Minnesota Press,
2037 University Avenue Southeast,
Minneapolis, Minnesota 55414

Library of Congress Cataloging in Publication Data

Bernard, Richard M   1948-
   The melting pot and the altar.

   Bibliography: p.
   Includes index.
   1. Marriage-Wisconsin. 2. Marriage Mixed-
Wisconsin. 3. Minorities-Wisconsin. 4. Assimilation
(Sociology) I. Title
HQ536.B48   306.8'09775   80-16287
ISBN 0-8166-0988-8

For
Terry Bowman Bernard

Acknowledgments

My research on intermarriage in Wisconsin had its unlikely beginnings on a warm February afternoon in 1974 in the Texas State Archives at Austin. I had gone to Texas the previous fall to study geographic mobility patterns in Houston and Dallas, only to discover that the topic belonged in the field of medical research as a cure for insomnia. In an idle moment, I fingered through some dusty county marriage registers dating to the days of the Texas Republic. At the time, I was only seeking a way to trace the movements of women whose names changed when they married, but I quickly became interested in the marriage records themselves and in the information that they contained. I began to see them as prime documents for studying social interactions, and I began to mull over the seemingly innocent questions of "Who married whom?" and "Why?" I began thinking of marriage as a measure of acceptance. Groups who intermarried accepted one another. The study of marriage patterns—what an excellent means for understanding group assimilation! I thought of my adopted state of Wisconsin with its great pool of European immigrants, and I wondered whether it would be possible to understand immigrant assimilation there through an examination of that state's central marriage registry. Suddenly I realized that I was considering a much larger concept than I had first thought: not simply the altar, but the American melting pot as well. From that moment, I knew I would return to Wisconsin. I went home that afternoon and searched through the storage bin for my overcoat.

Between that time and this, I have incurred more than the usual number of debts to individuals and organizations. I greatly appreciate the friendship and technical advice extended to me by Professors Stanley K. Schultz and John B. Sharpless of the University of Wisconsin and the methodological help which I received from Charles Palit and Jane Neice of the Survey Research Center and Gordon Caldwell and David Dickens of the Center for Demography and Ecology, both at Wisconsin. Similarly, I wish to thank Professors Shultz, Sharpless, and Allan G. Bouge of Wisconsin, John Modell of Minnesota, and Timothy Tackett of Catholic University for criticizing earlier versions of this work. Whatever weaknesses remain result from my failure to listen to their advice more closely.

I am also grateful to the National Science Foundation, the Newberry Library and the Marquette University Graduate School for funding my efforts. A National Science Foundation grant made it possible for James C. Schneider, Anthony C. Polvino, and George Sweet to assist me in data collection and processing. Without their good humor and fellowship, I would not have survived the tedium inherent in quantitative research. A grant from the Newberry enabled me to examine both their collections and the 1900 United States census manuscripts at the Chicago Federal Records Center. My thanks go to Professors Richard Jensen and Daniel Scott Smith. Money from Marquette made possible a summer of interviews and manuscript refinement. In addition, I appreciate the efforts of Professor John D. Buenker and his students at the University of Wisconsin-Parkside in helping me to gather materials on Racine residents. Similarly, the staff of the State Historical Society of Wisconsin, and especially reference librarian James Hansen, deserve my thanks for guiding me to numerous materials on Wisconsin's history. Equally deserving are Tony Polvino, George and Elaine Sweet, Peter and Marsha Cannon, Mary Weddig, and Terry Bernard for helping me keypunch during moments of crisis. I greatly appreciate all of these efforts.

I save a special word of thanks for three people, my wife Terry, my mother Elizabeth C. Bernard, and my good friend Bradley R. Rice for their many years of support. Of these, I wish to single out Terry for her consistent and invaluable encouragement. Her confidence and assistance over the last ten years have meant everything to me. This book is for her.

Contents

Introduction

The Study

of Marital Assimilation

Charles A. Sandburg and Lillian A. Steichen married in Milwaukee on June 15, 1908. The public record listed the groom as a 30-year-old "party organizer," born in Illinois, the son of Swedish parents. The bride, a school teacher residing in Menomonee Falls, Wisconsin, was the Michigan-born daughter of a Luxembourger couple, John P. and Mary Steichen. Mr. Carl Thompson performed the ceremony, and Mrs. Olive S. Gaylord and Mrs. Kate Thompson witnessed the event. What the official documents cannot show, however, is why Carl and "Paula" Sandburg fell in love and married.[1]

Less than a month before the young couple met, Carl Sandburg, a ne'er-do-well lecturer and poet from Galesburg, Illinois, was working as an editorial writer for a Chicago journal called the *Lyceumite*. In that capacity, he met Winfield R. Gaylord, the principal state organizer for Wisconsin's Social-Democratic Party, who had come to the Windy City on a visit. Gaylord talked with the young writer about the party and its future plans and encouraged him to come to Wisconsin and join in the socialist efforts. Sandburg, who had long since given up the Republicanism of his father for the prairie Populism of William Jennings Bryan, was ready for such new directions. Immediately he wrote to party officials in Milwaukee, and soon he was on his way to the Badger State to begin his career as a "rabble rouser."[2] Before the end of the same month, in fact, he established a base in Oshkosh and began work in the Fox River Valley and Lake Shore Districts.

Over the Christmas holidays Sandburg journeyed to party head-quarters at Brisbane Hall in Milwaukee. As it happened, a young school teacher, Lillian Steichen, was there conferring with party chief Victor Berger over her English translations of Berger's German-language editorials. Miss Steichen, who taught at Princeton, Illinois, Township High School, had come to Milwaukee from her parents' farm in Menomonee Falls, where she was spending her winter vacation.

The first impression that Paula (a name Carl would soon give her) had of the new organizer was that of a "gaunt and worn" young man. She initially thought of him only in terms of the party: She hoped that he could help the socialist cause, but she worried that he was working himself too hard.[3] She did, however, allow Sandburg to escort her home, only to refuse his invitation for dinner. "In those days things were different," she later recalled. "No really nice girl would have dinner with someone she just met."[4] Nonetheless, he persisted, and they began a correspondence that by springtime blossomed into romance.

When Paula wrote that she would be spending her Easter break with her family, Carl invited himself to join her in Menomonee Falls.[5] Her family was less than thrilled: Here was a full-grown man with a salary of only twenty-five dollars a month (and even that paid irregularly), who was full of radical ideas, quotations from Shakespeare, and unpublished poetry. He was not the sort of fellow a hard-working, middle-class farm family welcomed with open arms. Fortunately, Paula's brother, photographer Edward Steichen, favored the match and helped dispel the parents' fears.

Carl and Paula married in June in a civil ceremony more remi-niscent of the initialing of some public contract than a recitation of the traditional vows. No clergyman was present; instead, Social-ist party information director Thompson officiated. His wife and Mrs. Gaylord were among the few present. There were no rings, and the word "obey" went unspoken. The bride and groom simply agreed to a joint partnership, readily dissolvable by either party — an option never exercised during the 59-year life of the pact. After the wedding, the two political organizers rented an apartment in Appleton, Wisconsin, and set about the business of ordering their new home.[6]

The marriage of Carl Sandburg and Paula Steichen follows the traditional notion of an "American melting pot." Only in America, so we once thought, could this sort of thing happen. Here, the son of Swedish immigrants could override parental objections and wed the daughter of Luxembourgers. For Carl and Paula, it was apparently unimportant that they came from different nationalities; indeed, they may have hardly realized that fact. Their similarities in such things as background, temperament, and beliefs clearly overrode any ethnic considerations. And, this fact, after all, is central to the notion of a melting pot that supposedly produced a "blending American."[7]

Objectives

Regardless of their seemingly all-American courtship, the Sandburgs could not — nor indeed, could any single couple or group of individuals — reflect the marital patterns of a state or nation. This study, therefore, picks up where such individualized accounts stop. It combines the experiences of a large number of married couples from Wisconsin, in hopes of discovering the rates and patterns of marital assimilation in the Badger State. It examines, not two nationalities, but 11 such groups, and the brides and grooms within them, with the intent of discovering important factors that promoted intermarriages.

Since the pioneer work of sociologist Julius Drachsler over a half-century ago, scholars have recognized the importance of intermarriage as an indicator of the assimilation of European immigrants into American society.[8] Writing in 1920, Drachsler labeled intermarriage the "severest test of group cohesion" and called for a gathering of statistics to "furnish concrete, measurable materials in the field where such data are as urgently needed as they are hard to secure."[9] Since that time, social scientists have scoured city records for contemporary evidence of marriages across racial and religious barriers, but relatively few scholars have focused on the original "melting pot" concept of the assimilation of Europeans and their children during the pre-World War I era.

In recent years, social historians, less concerned with the assimilation process than with the problems of community development, have written a number of excellent case studies centering on one or more immigrant subsocieties within several American cities.[10] In emphasizing the pluralistic side of immigrant life, these works stressed the viability of family structures and community institutions in the face of substantial social, political, and geographic mobility within immigrant neighborhoods.

Although these studies covered many such vital matters, they gave less attention to equally important questions involving minority-majority relationships, both within and beyond the bounds of individual metropolitan areas. Yet these relationships, or more specifically their assimilative influences, may well have been as crucial to the survival of immigrant groups as were the groups' internal activities. The intent of this study, therefore, is to shed new light on immigrant assimilation by centering attention on the extent, patterns, and causes of intermarriage.

As a background for understanding marital assimilation patterns, Chapter 1 surveys Wisconsin's major immigrant groups, focusing especially on a number of demographic and socioeconomic factors that may have affected those patterns. Chapter 2 then presents the intermarriage rates *per se,* giving due regard to the differences between those of first- and second-generation immigrants and between those of persons from metropolitan and nonmetropolitan areas. Chapters 3 and 4 analyze several important demographic and socioeconomic characteristics of individual marriers and their groups, factors that allegedly affected mate selection across group lines. Although this study makes no pretense of explaining why particular couples such as Carl and Paula Sandburg married, it does attempt to show the rates at which members of different national groups intermarried and to analyze a number of influences on their decision-making.

The state of Wisconsin proves ideal for such a study. Owing to its large immigrant population and its reputation for progressive social attitudes, this state, if any area, should certainly have exemplified the American "melting pot." Although the data surveyed stretch from roughly the date of Wisconsin's admission to the union (1848) to the passage of the National Immigration Act of 1921, the primary focus is on the immediate pre-World War I era. Within this context, it is possible to examine marital assimilation in both metropolitan and nonmetropolitan environments during the flood tide of American immigration.

The comparative statistical data presented here derive primarily from the manuscripts of Wisconsin's state marriage registrations for decennial years 1890-1920. General samples drawn from each of these years, along with intensive samples of the state and the cities of Milwaukee and Racine in 1910, provide the base of information. These manuscripts usually reported the bride's and groom's names, birthplaces, and residences before marriage and the names of their parents. For a single decade, 1907-17, they also carried vital information on the birthplaces of the couple's parents. Generally, the man's occupation appeared, but often, especially in the earlier years, the records simply show the bride as being "at home" or as "keeping house" or, in fact, as having no occupation at all.[11]

The manuscript federal censuses of 1850-80 also have contributed to this work, but the value of these sources is limited. These supposedly listed all individuals married within one year prior to the census date. The 1850 data, for example, should have included all persons who married between June 1, 1849, and May 31, 1850, and who were living with their spouses at the latter date. Unfortunately, however, these data suffered from both restrictive questioning and marked underreporting so severe as to preclude their extensive use.[12]

The importance of such data lies in the value of intermarriage as a measure of the success of the American melting pot. Better described as a concept than as a theory, the term "melting pot" means an assimilated society in which people from a variety of cultural backgrounds have so intermingled as to form a new people, distinct from their forebears. The existence of a melting pot implies a mutual acceptance among groups that causes intense interactions, leading to a dissolution of separate identities and a merger into one body.[13]

The origins of the concept may be traced as far back as 1782, when French traveler J. Hector St. Jean de Crévecoeur asked, "What is the American, this new man?" Many since have concluded with de Crévecoeur that he is a "promiscuous breed"—in the Frenchman's time, "a mixture of English, Scotch, Irish, French, Dutch, Germans and Swedes" who intermarried and produced a hybrid offspring. De Crévecoeur used the term "melted" to describe the process of amalgamation that he felt created the American people.[14]

More than a century passed, however, before the concept of an American melting pot came into vogue. Although nineteenth-century Americans who resided near Germans, Irish, and other foreign groups were well aware of, and sometimes antagonistic toward, their presence, the nation as a whole took less notice of these early arrivals than it did of those who came later. Not until the great migrations of Eastern and Southern European Catholics and Jews in the years around the turn of the century did the majority of native-stock Americans begin to assess their new neighbors. Only then did native spokesmen formulate plans for immigrant absorption into the American mainstream. The ironically timed appearance of Israel Zangwill's emotion-charged stage play, *The Melting Pot,* in 1908 gave currency to the notion of an assimilated society at the time when its native component was becoming uneasy over the mixture. The popularity of the melting pot as a concept gave way to the "nativism" that forced the establishment of immigration quotas in the early 1920s. By the Coolidge era, the melting pot was an idea whose time had passed, a victim of nativist claims that the so-called "new immigrants" would never melt in the American crucible.[15]

Such a judgment was premature, since in most respects modern-day descendants of European immigrants are fully assimilated into American life. Of course there are exceptions, but by and large, Poles and Italians have blended into American society, as did the Germans and Irish before them. The processes may have differed and certainly the timing was not the same, but each of these groups has experienced substantial intermixture. Thus, the key question is not whether assimilation occurred, but to what extent it had progressed by a given time, and what factors promoted or retarded its development? If there were differences among groups, what caused those differences? Among individuals, who were the most likely to assimilate and lessen their group ties? Why these persons and not others?

Answering these questions depends on the measurement of assimilation, a vague and elusive term at best. How can one tell if a person is assimilated into his or her new environment? One means is to identify the number of people in each group who chose marriage partners from other groups.

Intermarriage, while certainly not the only indicator of immigrant assimilation, provides an excellent means of measuring such interactions. Regardless of its exact relationship to the mixing process, whether as cause, effect, or partner, intergroup matrimony is intrinsically bound to the process of intergroup assimilation.

Assimilation, defined according to the rigorous criteria that the groups in question become totally indistinguishable, clearly implies that intermarriage has occurred. Only by biological interaction — amalgamation — could the members of separate groups dissolve all differences, physical as well as cultural, and "melt" into one homogeneous compound. As a requirement for such a mixture, therefore, intermarriage is a suitable measure of the degree of interaction.

Yet even under the more relaxed notion of assimilation as social similarity and integration, intermarriage remains an important measuring device. One sociologist, Milton M. Gordon, for example, has argued that amalgamation insures a causal link between structural mixing and mutual acceptance by disparate groups.[16] For Gordon (see below), intermarriage guaranteed that other forms of social intercourse will follow. Other scholars have tied marital assimilation as either cause or effect to such assimilative phenoena as residential integration, lower levels of group identity, and greater understandings of the cultures of other people.[17] Thus, regardless of whether it plays the role of chicken or egg, intermarriage offers a resonable means of detecting assimilative activity.

Mixed marriages, moreover, carry two additional advantages over other evidences of assimilation. First, from a practical standpoint, intermarriage is readily identifiable. Unlike such elusive indicators as the adoption of native dress and speech patterns or membership in native social organizations, matrimonial bonds are a matter of public record. From such listings, researchers can derive marital assimilation rates, readily comparable to one another in numeric terms. Second, intermarriage is a widely accepted criteria. Most, if not all, social scientists have long recognized intermarriage as "perhaps the most conclusive indicator of the degree of assimilation of the minority."[18] In fact, the only direct objection against the linkage of intermarriage and assimilation that has received much attention in the literature was that of Simon Marcson in 1950.[19] Marcson argued that intermarriage, which he claimed was a function of class similarities, was not a pure index of assimilation. "A group," he insisted, "may become assimilated without showing a high rate of intermarriage. . . . A group may acquire the memories, sentiments, and attitudes of other groups and at the same time restrict its mate selection."[20]

This same intermarriage literature, however, has regarded Marcson's comments rather lightly—perhaps because of the confusion in his work between integration and assimilation. Most authorities think of the former as a mixture of people with separate groupings still distinguishable within it (a condition that Marcson seems to have labeled as "assimilation"). Yet assimilation, by definition, goes farther and extinguishes those differences.[21] After demonstrating that Marcson's critique applied only to intermarriage as a test of integration, demographers C. A. Price and J. Zubrzycki concluded that:

> For an assessment of integration, marriage patterns may be quite irrelevant—here Marcson is obviously right—but for complete assimilation, intermarriage is still a most useful index since a high rate of intermarriage results in a situation where descendants of immigrant families become so mixed up with descendants of other immigrant stock that they are virtually indistinguishable.[22]

In short, intermarriage rates provide one of the most reliable, most readily available, and most widely accepted means of measuring assimilation.

Theory and Methods

Several major problems, the first theoretical and the others methodological, confront the researcher who wishes to learn about assimilation by examining marriage records. At the theoretical level it is necessary to construct a causative framework accounting for the major factors that encouraged intermarriage. This framework, when presented in the form of an equation, should include inter-marriage as the dependent variable under the influence of both group-related and individual factors.

In such an analysis, it is necessary to treat intermarriage as a separate item and not simply as a reflection of the strength of endogamy as a norm for certain groups. Worried that researchers of his era (1941) were employing the former to define the latter, sociologist Robert K. Merton developed a simple typology for understanding the relationship between them.[23] According to Merton, the frequency of intermarriage depended on the inter-action of two factors: norms (all kinds) and conditions. Norms, he suggested, could be either prescriptive or proscriptive, either en-couraging or discouraging to in-group or out-group marriage. Such norms might control intermarriage either directly (that is, by pro-scribing or, at least in theory, by prescribing it) or indirectly. In the latter case, norms become advisory and result in "permissive, preferential and assortative" mating. These direct and indirect norms then interact with circumstances or "conditions" that control the availability of prospective mates, such as the sizes and the sex and age compositions of the groups in question, along with the degree of contact between their members; such conditions could hamper the ability of norms to regulate behavior.

All this interaction seems simple enough to understand, but it is incomplete. Where, for example, is the tie between intermarriage and assimilation? Where is there an allowance for the old saw that "like marries like," or, indeed, for its contradictory counterpart, "opposites attract"? Where does personal preference come into the picture?

Milton Gordon has suggested a highly plausible answer to the first of these questions by linking "structural assimilation" to intermarriage and, through it, to other types of assimilation.[24] Rather than expounding his theory in terms of norms and condi-tions, Gordon focused on cultural and structural assimilation. Cul-tural assimilation, or acculturation, usually comes first, according to this version, but there is no guarantee of general assimilation until structured interaction also develops. This structural inter-action, if it emerges at all, either follows or coincides with acculturation. It is, in effect, an intermixing that involves the "large-scale entrance into cliques, clubs, and institutions of the host society on a primary-group level." Although no necessary link exists between acculturation and the other assimilative processes, structural mixing, according to Gordon, unavoidably leads to intermarriage. This eventuality brings about an end to discrimination and prejudice, or in Gordon's terms, "behavioral and attitudinal assimilation," and results in complete intermixing.

Perhaps because of its clarity, Gordon's theory remains dominant in the field, but it does have certain drawbacks that detract from its appeal. The theory itself presents a mechanistic approach to intermarriage, placing little value on changing norms, beliefs, and values, as represented in part by the term "acculturation." Gordon, moreover, allows no room for the largely immeasurable personal preferences of individuals that may on occasion subvert his structural analysis. The problem then is to construct a theory of marital assimilation that accounts for each of these factors.

In theoretical terms, therefore, intermarriage between groups represents a breakdown in the endogamy norm, a circumstance most likely where there is integration involving primary relationships. Such interaction itself results from three factors: First, the desire to intermingle must be strong, that is, people in one group must feel attracted to those in another. Such attraction usually develops when the parties in question have things in common, when they share similar traits. Thus, the greater the number of people from two or more groups who share certain characteristics, the more likely that the groups will interact and that intermarriages will occur. Second, conditions must be conducive to mixture. Not only must the receiving group be willing and able to accept outsiders, but the outsiders must know about such opportunities. In effect, interaction and intermarriage are more likely where one group wants outsiders (where they need outsiders as marriage partners, for example) and where the outsiders have contact with these groups and thus know of the options offered. Third, personal preferences should no more discourage than encourage mixing and intermarriage. Unfortunately, there is no way to evaluate such preferences other than through a case-by-case study. The researcher cannot determine, for example, whether all the "handsome" boys and "pretty" girls of a given community belonged to only one group, a circumstance that would have increased the desirability of those people as marriage partners. "Handsome" and "pretty" are subjective concepts. Intermarriage studies can only assume that such factors cancel out in a macro-level, statewide study.

Thus, aside from the individual quirks that defy broad generalization, intermarriage — a breakdown of the endogamous norms — results from two factors conducive to integration: the desire to intermingle, and the availability of opportunities for interaction together with the knowledge of those opportunities. Since such knowledge depends on contact, these factors might be restated as (1) the exposure of individuals to cultures other than their own; and (2) the relative availability of similar, marriageable people in other groups, as measured by both their total numbers and their social desirability. The incidence of intermarriage, therefore, should have increased for persons with relatively wider cultural contacts and for those who found potential mates in other groups to be both more abundant and more similar to themselves than those from their own groups.

Testing this theory involves the careful handling of several methodological problems, beginning with the question of geographic scope. Over the last half-century, social scientists have produced an impressive number of case studies of intermarriages in communities widely scattered across the country.[25] Unfortunately, few of these researchers extracted data from beyond the confines of their chosen cities, and thus the usefulness of their findings for generalizations about immigrant experiences remains highly restricted. Without corroborative work on other locations, there is little way of knowing how representative these urban areas were of their own states or of the nation as a whole.[26]

Perhaps the best illustration of the problem of representativeness lies in the development of Ruby Jo Reeves Kennedy's famous "triple melting pot" thesis of ethnic out-marriage along religious lines.[27] With the possible exception of Drachsler's book on New York City, no work has received more attention in the intermarriage literature than Kennedy's several publications on exogamy in New Haven, Connecticut, 1870-1950. As a pioneering contribution to the field, Kennedy's findings deserve much credit. Nonetheless, as reflections of conditions beyond that New England city, her results are woefully inadequate.

For Kennedy, the main concern was not the rate at which people out-married, but rather the rules they followed in choosing their mates. From her limited data base, she skillfully demonstrated that in New Haven, most ethnic out-marriages were religiously endogamous, a situation resulting in the creation, not of a single "melting pot" but instead, of three bubbling caldrons: one each for Protestants, Catholics, and Jews.

Unfortunately for scholars, such as Will Herberg and Milton Gordon, who employed Kennedy's findings in their own work, New Haven proved to be a poor location for study. In fact, a contemporary of Kennedy's, John L. Thomas, used diocesan records from across the country to demonstrate that Catholics rarely followed her rules.[28] In this aspect of mate selection, New Haven proved atypical, not only of the nation, but even of the state of Connecticut.[29]

The second methodological problem, one of deciding just which rates to report, centers on the definition of a "rate." It is the percentage of intermarriages (that is, of couples who intermarried), or is it the percentage of people who intermarried? Hyman Rodman gave the following example to illustrate the problem:

> If we have six homogamous Catholic marriages and four mixed Catholic marriages, we can speak of either a 40% or a 25% mixed marriage rate. Four of the ten marriages or 40% of the marriages involving Catholics, are mixed, but four Catholics out of 16, or 25%, are in mixed marriages.[30]

Rodman further observed that the famous debate between Thomas and A. B. Hollingshead, wherein the former reported an intermarriage rate for Catholics in New Haven of 40% and the latter claimed that 6% was the real figure, foundered on this difference. Thomas' was a rate for marriages while Hollingshead's was for individuals. Converting Thomas' figure to an individual rate of 25% did not solve the dispute, but it did bring the combatants much closer together.[31]

Price and Zubrzycki, however, recognized a set of more serious methodological problems in defining mate selection.[32] Initially, they indicated the inconsistency between ethnic groupings and and groups based on birthplace or nationality. The present study skirts that issue by frankly concentrating on national-origin groups and thus avoids the term "ethnic group" almost entirely. Such an approach, the only one feasible for a statewide analysis of small groups, circumvents but admittedly does not eliminate the impact of subgroups, particularly Jews, on intermarriage statistics.

The alternative to such a method is an artificial clustering of the immigrant groups in some manner similar to that of Edmund de S. Brunner. Brunner's *Immigrant Farmers and Their Children,* now a classic in rural sociology, included a well-documented chapter on intermarriage.[33] The study, which covered the years 1908-1925, used data from marriage applications from 60 all-rural or nearly all-rural counties of Nebraska and 29 and 21 such areas in New York and Wisconsin, respectively.

In his work, Brunner deliberately and uniquely combined all of the foreign groups into "racial" (cultural or linguistic) categories: Anglo-Saxons, Scandinavians, Teutons, Slavs, and Latins. Thus, for Brunner, Czech-German matches were intermarriages across ethnic lines, but Czech-Russian pairings were not. The results of this procedure were indeed unfortunate. While greatly underutilizing his enormous samples, Brunner isolated his findings from comparisons with all other studies, both rural and nonrural. Even then, Brunner failed to counter the effects on out-marriage rates caused by the major ethnic subgroup, Jews.

A second problem that Price and Zubrzycki posed concerns the difference between sociological generations and birthplace categories. Essentially, they argued that people who immigrated while they were still under 12 years of age behaved like second-generation immigrants because they spent their formative years within their new environments. Without data on year of immigration or age at debarkation, a statewide study simply cannot handle this problem and thus must accept this disadvantage in order to move beyond the case-study level. Since most immigrants were young adults, not small children, the authors may, however, have overstated the seriousness of the charge.

Finally, the most important problem cited by Price and Zybrzycki was the identification of the population at risk of intermarriage.[34] This issue centers on the place in which the marriage actually occurred. The standard method of rate selection involves identification of those who married in the given locale (in this case the state of Wisconsin) as the population (at risk). This method, however, results in an undercount of males and an overstatement of their intermarriage rates and also causes an overcount of females and an underestimate of their out-marriage rates. The reasons for these errors are somewhat complex. An undetermined number of male immigrants returned to their countries of origin for brides, or married in those countries by proxy, and thus missed enumeration as endogamous marriers. At the same time, females who came to America for the purpose of marrying (called "wharfside brides" by Price and Zybrzycki) counted as having been at risk of intermarriage when they should not have, since they contracted for endogamous matches before arrival in the United States.

The Price-Zubrzycki solution was a "survival index," like those used by sociologists Paul C. Glick and Paul H. Besanceney.[35] This measure counted all married couples at a given place and time regardless of the location or date of their weddings.[36]

In rebuttal to Price and Zubrzycki, Stanley Lieberson countered that, if anything, a survival index was less reliable than the standard index based on simple tallies of marriages that occurred in a specific area over a certain period of time.[37] "Wharfside brides," he noted, appear in both measures, but at least the standard method excludes women "married in their homelands through proxies or by temporary visitors." In regard to the men, Lieberson suggested that exclusion of proxy marriers was justified since they usually arranged marriages before coming to America and thus did not "risk" intermarriage anyway. He further contended that men who married at wharfside, and thus counted on the American marriage rolls, counterbalanced those who returned home for their nuptials.

Lieberson concluded his argument by comparing the errors of the indexes of marital assimilation. Price and Zybrzycki's survivor index properly deflated intermarriage rates by including endogamous visit marriages, but it also improperly lowered rates still farther by the inclusions of both proxy and wharfside weddings. The standard index, on the other hand, rightly excluded proxy marriages and produced counteracting errors in regard to wharfside and visit marriages. Whereas the standard index included wharfside weddings—causing a tendency to underestimate intermarriage rates—it at the same time excluded visit marriages—resulting in an opposing tendency toward overestimation of the same rates. The relative merits of the two methods, therefore, depend on whether the double undercount of the survivor index exceeds the difference between the undercounts and overcounts of the standard method.

One alternative to both survivor and standard indexes is worthy of special attention. This final method of rate selection originated in sociologist Niles Carpenter's outstanding census monograph, *Immigrants and Their Children, 1920,* and its importance lies in Carpenter's attempt to use the method to develop nationwide rates of intermarriage.[38] In a chapter on that subject, Carpenter illustrated mate selection by examining the birthplaces of the parents of all persons enumerated in the federal census. Thus, the marriages scrutinized in his study were not those of the individuals canvassed, but those of their parents.

Carpenter's strategy, however, created a number of problems. Like Price and Zybrzycki's procedure, this approach caused the inclusion of many people who were never "at risk" of intermarriage in America and resulted in a consolidation of all marriages, without regard to time or immigrant generation. The marriages in question might have occurred one, ten, twenty, or even a hundred years prior to the census date—a situation that blocks all study of the changes in intermarriage patterns over time. Similarly, such an approach prohibits research into matches involving second-generation immigrants, since Carpenter could not separate these people (the parents of those on the census rolls) from native-stock Americans simply on the basis of their birthplaces.[39] To analyze mate selections among second-generation immigrants, Carpenter would have needed to know the birthplaces of the married couples' parents, that is, the grandparents of the individuals who actually appeared in the census. Finally, differential fertility and mortality and changes in location may have distorted Carpenter's findings, since his sample depends on the survival of the couples' children and the appearance of those children in the enumeration roles. If German couples, for instance, gave birth to more children, had children who lived longer than the offspring of couples from other groups, or simply had more children who migrated to the United States, the German marriages (and their corresponding in-marriage and out-marriage rates) would have had an undue influence on the conclusions that Carpenter drew.

Unfortunately, these difficulties are inherent in any similar manipulations of the census material on parentage, and thus they preclude for the present any nationwide analysis of intermarriage. This study, therefore, focuses instead on the statewide level, and owing to Lieberson's comparison of the survival and standard indexes of intermarriage, makes use of the standard methological approach of including only those who married in Wisconsin within a given year.

"Intermarriage," sociologist Lowery Nelson has written, "is a test of the strength or weakness of . . . prejudices and must therefore be regarded as a final test of assimilation."[40] By responding to Drachsler's half-century-old call for "measurable materials," this study should provide a new perspective on de Crévecoeur's well-known characterization of the United States as a place where "individuals of all nations are melted into a new race of man, whose labors and posterity will one day cause great changes in the world."[41] What better site for a reevaluation of the forgotten "American melting pot" than at the marriage altar?

The
Melting Pot
and the Altar

CHAPTER 1

Wisconsin's Immigrants

The central element in the social environment of Wisconsin during the first seven decades of its statehood was a substantial influx of European immigrants.[1] The easy accessibility of the state by ship across the Great Lakes and by rail via Chicago made it one of the major recipients of German and Scandinavian newcomers and a significant receiver of East European immigrants as well, especially those from the old Russian and Austrian empires. Throughout the censuses of the nineteenth century, over 30% of Wisconsin's residents listed foreign birthplaces, and despite a slow but steady decline in the proportion of foreign-born from 36% in 1850, a full 28% of the state's 1910 popluation was still composed of newcomers from abroad. Not until the following decade did the percentage drop significantly in a single 10-year period. If second-generation immigrants are added to the foreign-born totals, however, native-stock Americans were in a decided minority. Between 1870 and 1910, persons of foreign stock consistently comprised about 70% of Wisconsin's population.[2]

Although the people from these nationalities all shared in the common experience of adaptation to life in the American Midwest, their groups differed considerably in their social characteristics.

3

Some groups tended toward rural settlement while others made new homes in the city; some included large numbers of people — enough to dominate particular areas — but others remained quite small; some boasted of large middle and upper classes when others had few members outside the working class. Such geographic, demographic, and socioeconomic differences could have greatly affected the groups' patterns of marital assimilation. More specifically, residential choices (particularly as they related to immigrant clustering and community size), sex ratios, and marriage-age patterns, as well as such factors as occupations and religious preferences, may well have either restricted or enhanced the likelihood of intermarriage. Thus, an understanding of crossgroup mating begins with a knowledge of the groups themselves.

Immigration

Easily the largest immigrant group throughout the period was the Germans. Their numbers peaked at over three-quarters of a million in 1910, representing over a third of the total population of Wisconsin in each census from 1880 to the First World War. In the early years, 1850-1880, the second and third groups in size were the British (English, Scots, and Welsh) and the Irish, who, together with a large proportion of the Canadians, made English-speaking immigrants a significant factor in the overall population mix. Thereafter, Norwegians were the second largest, though Poles surpassed their first-generation total in 1920. The combination of Norwegians, Swedes, and Danes pushed the Scandinavian figure over 250,000 (10% of the total population in that year). Together, the countries of Czechoslovakia, Poland, Russia, Austria, Hungary, and Italy probably accounted for over 320,000 people in the 1920 population of 2.6 million.[3] Whereas Eastern and Southern Europeans represented only 5% of the 1870 first-generation total, their proportion grew by 1920 to about 30% of those born abroad.

Before statehood, early British settlers scattered across the southern quarter of Wisconsin in search of either homesteads or employment in the newly opened lead mines in the southwest.[4] In 1850, for example, the only counties with 2,000 or more English, whose whole number (18,952) comprised 70% of the British tally,

Table 1.1. Population of Wisconsin by County of Birth from 1850 to 1920

	1850	1860	1870	1880
Total	305,391	775,881	1,054,670	1,315,497
White	304,756	774,710	1,051,351	1,309,618
(%)	(99.8)[b]	(99.8)	(99.7)	(99.6)
Native	194,914	498,980	686,903	910,072
	(63.8)	(64.3)	(65.1)	(69.1)
Of U.S. Parents	...	...	33,570	364,348
	...	...	(31.6)	(27.7)
Of Foreign Parents	...	...	353,333	545,724
	...	...	(33.5)	(41.5)
Foreign	110,477	276,901	364,448	405,425
	(36.2)	(35.7)	(34.6)	(30.8)
Great Britain[c]	26,798	43,923	41,522	36,150
Ireland	21,043	49,961	48,479	41,907
Canada	8,277	...	25,666	28,965[d]
Germany	38,064	125,798	162,314	184,328
Switzerland	1,244	4,732	6,069	6,283
Norway	8,651	21,442	40,046	49,349
Sweden	88	673	2,799	8,138
Denmark	146	1,150	5,212	8,797
Poland	...	417	1,290	5,263
Russia	71	95	102	312
Bohemia	...	...	10,570	13,848
Austria	61	7,081	4,486	4,601
Hungary	...	...	237	447
Italy	9	103	104	253
Other	6,023	11,662	15,639	16,784
Nonwhite	635	1,171	3,319	5,879
(%)	(0.2)	(0.2)	(0.3)	(0.4)

Source: See text note 1.

[a]The 1890 second-generation immigrant figures represent total whites with foreign or mixed parents minus foreign-born whites.

[b]Numbers in parentheses are percentages.

[c]England, Scotland, and Wales.

[d]Figures are for British America.

[e]Includes Newfoundland.

[f]Figures are for Czechoslovakia.

Table 1.1, *continued*

	1890[a]	1900	1910	1920
Total	1,686,880	2,069,042	2,333,860	2,632,067
White	1,680,473	2,057,911	2,320,555	2,616,938
	(99.6)	(99.5)	(99.4)	(99.4)
Native	1,167,681	1,553,071	1,820,995	2,171,582
	(69.2)	(75.1)	(78.0)	(82.5)
Of U.S. parents	440,846	596,768	776,234	1,069,466
	(26.1)	(28.8)	(33.3)	(40.6)
Of foreign parents	726,835	956,303	1,044,761	1,102,116
	(43.1)	(46.2)	(44.8)	(41.9)
Foreign	519,199	515,971	512,865	460,485
	(30.8)	(24.9)	(28.0)	(17.5)
Great Britain	33,424	25,920	26,351	15,609
Ireland	33,306	23,544	14,049	7,809
Canada	33,163	33,951[e]	24,921	29,483[e]
Germany	259,819	242,777	201,592	151,250
Switzerland	7,181	7,666	8,036	7,797
Norway	65,696	61,575	56,999	45,433
Sweden	20,157	26,196	25,739	22,896
Denmark	13,885	16,171	16,454	15,420
Poland	17,660	31,789	51,090	50,558
Russia	2,279	4,243	15,545	21,447
Bohemia	11,999	14,145	...	19,811[f]
Austria	4,856	7,319	33,648	19,641
Hungary	486	1,123	10,554	10,016
Italy	1,123	2,172	9,273	11,188
Other	14,165	17,380	18,780	42,197
Nonwhite	6,407	11,131	13,305	15,029
	(0.4)	(0.5)	(0.6)	(0.6)

Table 1.2. Second-Generation Immigrants by National Origins in Wisconsin from 1880 to 1920 (with percentage of the Total Immigrant Group)

	1880	1890[a]	1900	1910	1920
Totals	951,149	1,246,034	1,472,008	1,557,330	1,562,601
First Generation	405,425	519,199	515,971	512,865	460,485
	(42.6)[b]	(41.7)	(35.0)	(32.9)	(29.5)
Second Generation	545,724	726,835	956,303	1,044,761	1,102,116
	(57.4)	(58.3)	(65.0)	(67.1)	(70.5)
Second Generation					
Great Britain[c]	59,265	59,454	59,982	53,902	49,301
	(62.1)	(64.0)	(69.8)	(72.6)	(76.0)
Ireland	84,167	80,043	71,323	60,786	51,295
	(66.8)	(70.6)	(75.2)	(81.2)	(86.8)
Canada	31,885[d]	27,766	58,151[e]	53,780	49,490[e]
	(52.4)	(45.6)	(63.2)	(70.6)	(77.9)
Germany	251,461	366,211	466,731	794,943	682,869
	(57.7)	(58.5)	(63.5)	(70.6)	(77.9)
Switzerland	...	...	10,780	12,840	15,153
	...	...	(58.4)	(61.5)	(66.0)
Norway		65,041	93,449	100,701	102,385
	Scandinavia[f]	(49.7)	(60.3)	(63.9)	(69.3)
Sweden	46,029	9,836	22,517	29,647	33,619
	(41.0)	(32.8)	(46.2)	(53.5)	(59.5)
Denmark		9,938	17,786	21,861	24,647
		(41.7)	(52.4)	(57.1)	(61.5)
Poland	...	...	42,927	...	...
	...	...	(57.5)	...	...
Russia	...	492	2,278	15,763	40,979
	...	(17.8)	(23.2)	(34.7)	(65.6)
Bohemia	...	13,728	...	...	...
	...	(53.4)	...	...	...
Austria	...	...	30,038	43,035	70,072
	...	...	(56.8)	(52.7)	(78.1)

Source: See text note 1.

[a]The 1890 second-generation immigrant figures represent total whites with foreign or mixed parents minus foreign-born whites.

[b]Figures in parentheses are percentages.

[c]England, Scotland, and Wales.

[d]Figures are for British America.

[e]Includes Newfoundland.

[f]Includes Finns.

[g]Native whites with parents born in different foreign countries.

Table 1.2, *continued*

	1880	1890[a]	1900	1910	1920
Hungary	...	8	813	2,612	11,207
	...	(1.6)	(42.0)	(19.8)	(52.8)
Italy	...	298	1,198	3,967	11,101
	...	(21.0)	(35.5)	(27.9)	(49.8)
Other	42,410	50,787	25,131	30,351	47,804
Mixed[g]	30,507	43,233	11,225	16,429	63,444

Table 1.3. Total Foreign Stock by National
Origins in Wisconsin from 1880 to 1920
(with percentage of the Total State Population)

	1880	1890[a]	1900	1910	1920
Totals	951,149	1,246,034	1,472,008	1,557,330	1,562,601
	(72.3)[b]	(73.9)	(71.1)	(66.7)	(58.2)
First Generation	405,425	519,199	515,971	512,865	460,485
	(30.8)	(30.8)	(24.9)	(28.0)	(17.5)
Second Generation	545,724	726,835	956,303	1,044,761	1,102,116
	(41.5)	(43.1)	(46.2)	(44.8)	(41.9)
First and Second Generations					
Great Britain[c]	95,415	92,878	85,899	74,252	64,910
	(7.3)	(5.5)	(4.2)	(3.2)	(2.5)
Ireland	126,074	113,349	94,867	74,835	59,104
	(9.6)	(6.7)	(4.6)	(3.2)	(2.2)
Canada	60,850[d]	60,929	92,063[e]	78,701	78,973[e]
	(4.6)	(3.6)	(4.4)	(3.4)	(3.0)
Germany	435,789	626,030	735,113	794,943	682,869
	(33.1)	(37.1)	(35.5)	(34.1)	(25.9)

Source: See text note 1.

[a] The 1890 second-generation immigrant figures represent total whites with foreign or mixed parents minus foreign-born whites.

[b] Figures in parentheses are precentages.

[c] England, Scotland, and Wales.

[d] Figures are for British America.

[e] Includes Newfoundland.

[f] Excludes Finns.

[g] Native whites with parents born in different foreign countries.

Table 1.3, *continued*

	1880	1890[a]	1900	1910	1920
Switzerland	...	...	18,445	20,876	22,950
	...	...	(0.9)	(0.9)	(0.9)
Norway		130,737	155,024	157,700	147,818
	Scandinavia[f]	(7.8)	(7.5)	(6.8)	(5.6)
Sweden	112,313	29,993	48,713	55,386	56,515
	(8.5)	(1.8)	(2.4)	(2.4)	(2.1)
Denmark		23,828	33,957	38,315	40,067
		(1.4)	(1.6)	(1.6)	(1.5)
Poland	...	...	74,716	...	...
	...	...	(3.6)	...	...
Russia	...	2,771	9,828	45,407	62,426
	...	(0.2)	(0.5)	(1.9)	(2.4)
Bohemia	...	25,727	...	...	...
	...	(1.5)	...	...	...
Austria	...	...	52,870	81,726	89,713
	...	...	(2.6)	(3.5)	(3.4)
Hungary	...	494	1,936	13,166	21,223
	...	(0.0)	(0.1)	(0.6)	(0.8)
Italy	...	1,421	3,370	13,240	22,289
	...	(0.1)	(0.2)	(0.6)	(0.9)
Other	90,201	83,774	53,229	53,429	150,300
Mixed second generation[g]	30,507	43,233	11,225	16,429	63,444

were those in the lead region: Iowa, Grant, and Lafayette.[5] The 3,527 Scots located primarily in the south central and southeastern counties of Columbia, Rock, Waukesha, and Milwaukee. The 4,319 Welsh spread from Iowa and Columbia Counties to Milwaukee's neighboring county of Racine, but north only as far as Winnebago and Fond du Lac Counties on the western shore of Lake Winnebago.[6] Despite the head start enjoyed by these former British subjects, however, their totals peaked in 1870, and the relative importance of their numbers declined thereafter.

Some of the British immigrants in the lead region were former tin miners from the Cornwall in southwest England.[7] These Cornishmen, called "Cousin Jacks" by the townspeople, dug their homes into the hillsides around Mineral Point, thus engendering for Wisconsin its nickname of the "Badger state," a better choice, as Robert C. Nesbit has pointed out, than the equally popular label for the people, "suckers."[8] Because of their lower social status many of these Cornish miners kept apart from the growing number of native-born farmers filtering into their area. With the discovery of gold in California, a large proportion of these Cornish people packed their belongings and headed west, but a minority of them remained. As the lead supply dwindled, they too turned to farming for their livelihood.

A number of Irish also migrated to the mining region, and a few stopped along the way in the central areas of the south, but by 1850, over 30% of them had settled in the southeastern counties of Milwaukee, Racine, and Kenosha.[9] Of the 6,535 Irish in these three counties, many of whom fled from the potato famine that began in 1846, 2,816 lived in the city of Milwaukee, and over a third of these inhabited the old Third Ward downtown.[10] As in the case of the British, the totals for the Irish-born declined after the 1870s.

Irish people came to Milwaukee in the early days of its settlement. Fifty-one of 451 household heads in the 1840 United States Census had Irish names, and in 1850, 15% of the city's population were natives of the Emerald Isle.[11] Over half of the men (55.7%) in 1850 worked as common laborers, though the proportion fell slightly (44.0%) a decade later. The second largest occupational category in both years was that of the small craftsmen and their

Map 1: Early Twentieth Century Wisconsin

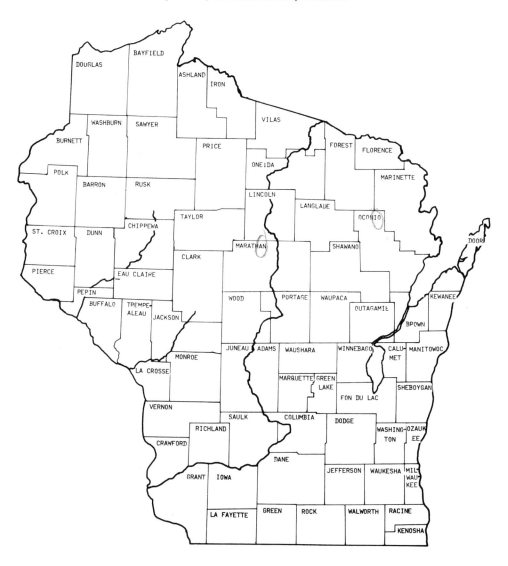

kindred workers (23.0% in 1850 and 27.8% in 1860). Although most Irish women worked in their own homes, some 450 of them in 1860 worked as maids in the houses of others.

Predominantly Catholic, Milwaukee's Irish struggled for many years with the more numerous German Catholics for control over the local diocese. With the Germans, they operated a number of parochial schools in either the English or German language, depending on the makeup of the particular parish. Much Irish social life centered on parish organizations such as fraternal groups, especially the Hibernian Benevolent Society and the Knights of St. Patrick, women's clubs, and temperance societies. In addition Irish militia units and literary and debating societies were formed. Weekly dances, visits to the neighborhood pubs (for the less temperately inclined), and celebrations, especially on St. Patrick's Day, however, probably did as much as any formal organization to hold the Irish community together.[12]

Although French Canadian fur traders had been the first white people to see Wisconsin, the total count of Canadians in the state at the federal census of 1850 was only slightly over 8,000. In no county did Canadians form as much as 10% of the total population, although identifiable groups of them did appear in Prairie du Chien on the Mississippi River in Crawford County, in Green Bay (Brown County), and in Fond du Lac and Milwaukee Counties.[13]

Individual Germans began filtering into Wisconsin in the early 1830s, but the mass migration, which raised talk of a "German state" in the Midwest, started in 1839.[14] In that year, Rev. Johannes A. A. Grabau persuaded some 800 "Old Lutherans" to abandon the doctrinal disputes of Prussia and journey to the developing territory of Wisconsin.[15] A flood of migrants followed between 1839 and 1846, and by 1850, one Wisconsinite in eight was a native of Germany. This in-movement, spurred by federal land sales and active promotion by the state government, reached its high points in 1853-1855 (about 16,000 came in 1854 alone), in 1866-1873, and again in 1880-1884, when nearly 20,000 Germans annually debarked in Milwaukee.[16] Only after 1890 did the census counts of German-born individuals begin to fall, and as late as 1920, Germans and their American-born children remained the most important foreign-origin component in the population.

Germans, who arrived before mid-century were concentrated in Milwaukee and Washington Counties, the latter then including present-day Ozaukee County. Substantial numbers of German farmers, however, skipped over these flatlands of the eastern shore-line and selected hilly and wooded inland properties, much like those of southern Germany. These men and their families supplied the bulk of the German populations (over 7,500 strong in 1850) in Fond du Lac, Dodge, and Jefferson Counties.[17] Later, as Map 2 displays, Germans moved farther west and north, eventually covering the whole state except the anglicized southern tier of counties and sparsely settled far north.

As early as 1850, and continuing through 1870, one-third of all Milwaukeeans were first-generation German immigrants, and throughout the nineteenth century, this proportion never fell below 25%. Germans of both generations filled the northwest third of the city and overflowed into the south side and east side wards as well. The group's huge size allowed the creation of a thoroughly German subsociety that prompted contemporaries to call the city the "German Athens."

Typical of the state's German settlers were the people from Lippe-Detmold who founded the village of Franklin in the Town of Herman, Sheboygan County, in 1847.[18] The majority to these people came to Wisconsin in search of better living conditions. In Lippe, so many generations had divided their lands among their sons that the tiny plots were no longer capable of supporting whole families. The Lippers, moreover, were Calvinists (members of the German Reformed Church) and had objected to the crown's ban on the Heidelberg Catechism, thus their emigration had a religious motivation as well. Combined, these two reasons proved such an impetus to emigration that by 1856 the original Liper settlement had grown to 300 to 400 people.

Most of these newcomers were farmers, though many entered trades, notably tailoring and carpentry. By the mid-1850s, the community included a sawmill, a gristmill, a blacksmith shop, a pottery, a tailor shop, a brewery, cooper shops, and saloons, and had a number of shopless artisans. The village of Franklin also produced several doctors and ministers and at least "a score of school teachers."[19]

Wages proved much better in America. A farmhand in Lippe earned only 15 to 30 dollars per year, with the average pay closer to the lower figure. A tailor received about the same amount; a

Map 2: Wisconsin Counties Having Large Immigrant Populations,
1850, 1880, and 1910

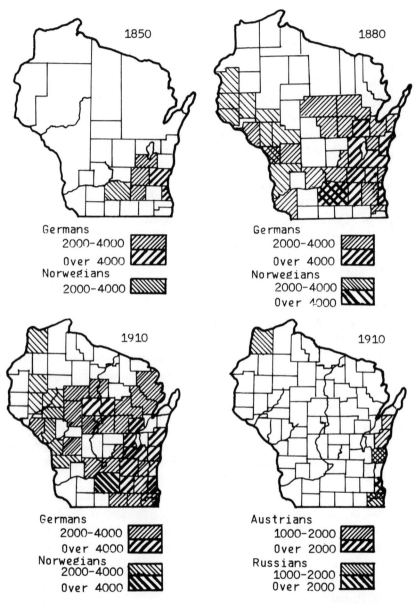

1850

Germans
2000-4000
Over 4000
Norwegians
2000-4000

1880

Germans
2000-4000
Over 4000
Norwegians
2000-4000
Over 4000

1910

Germans
2000-4000
Over 4000
Norwegians
2000-4000
Over 4000

1910

Austrians
1000-2000
Over 2000
Russians
1000-2000
Over 2000

SOURCES: Joseph Schafer, *A History of Agriculture in Wisconsin, Wisconsin Domesday Book,* Vol. I (Madison, 1922), Fig. 13, p. 50; U.S. Census, 1880, *Compendium,* Table XXXI, pp. 539-540; and U.S. Census, 1910, *Supplement for Wisconsin,* Table I, pp. 602-615.

carpenter made slightly more; a servant girl worked a whole year and in return earned $2.00 and some cloth from which to make her clothing. As one old settler put it, "And why should I have staid [*sic*] there when I knew that the prospects here were much better?"[20]

The journey to the United States, however, resulted in unexpected financial hazards. From the German port of Bremen to Sheboygan, the trip cost each person about $40.00 or over two years' wages for average working people (Bremen to Quebec, $32.00; Quebec to Buffalo, $5.00; Buffalo to Milwaukee, $2.50, with only a nominal fee for the last leg of the trip to Sheboygan). All travelers had to furnish their own food and prepare their own meals aboard ship. Then there were the baggage handling charges ("pier money") in Milwaukee. Dock workers in that city required that all luggage be placed on wagons. The use of each wagon came at a set fee of $5.00, which applied without exception, even if the last wagon held only one trunk. Moreover, the fee covered only the debarkation of the baggage on one dock. The immigrants had to pay the same amount to have their goods transferred to a steamer for Sheboygan. This rude welcome to their new home state caused such irritation among the Germans that the incident remained fresh in the minds of many, over 40 years later.

Overwhelmingly, these newcomers retained their allegiances to the German Reformed Church, and they built and supported two Reformed congregations in Herman. Each group maintained a parish school that functioned two months every year after the public schools recessed. Two other religious groups (Catholics and Lutherans) were represented in the town, but neither had many adherents.

The residents of Herman adopted American ways of dress (though some still wore wooden shoes as late as 1890), native institutions, and, in the second generation, the English language. Parents sent their children to the public school; the men voted in all elections.

Despite such outward evidences of assimilation, however, these Germans remained apart from other people for many years. Their needs were few, and so the settlement was able to care for its own people, interacting little with the rest of the county. In the early years, at least, theirs was a "complete community [with] . . . no need of seeking company outside their wide-spread settlement."[21]

The mass of Norwegians who poured into the Midwest after the American Civil War hardly paused in the eastern areas of Wisconsin.[22] The main desire of these travelers, who began arriving in the 1830s, was to own a family farm. In the early years, Norwegians homesteaded in Rock and Jefferson Counties and in Muskego in Waukesha County. While the latter group moved toward Racine, the former expanded north and west to create the Koshkonong community in Dane County. By 1860, another wave of newcomers made the Norwegians the largest foreign group in at least nine of the 12 counties on the western border of the state. By that time, however, the mainstream of Scandinavian migration had spanned the Mississippi and pushed into Minnesota and the Dakotas. Nonetheless, as Map 2 illustrates, the counties that Norwegians, as well as Germans, first chose later became the centers of much broader settlements within the Badger state.

The Norwegians of the town of Unity in Portage County were typical of their group. Like their German counterparts, they came to this country for economic reasons.[23] In the coastal areas of their homeland, Norwegian men working as lumbermen and farm laborers earned only 20 to 35 cents per day. Servant girls gained 8 to 15 dollars and some cloth annually. Even though the cost of living in Wisconsin was about twice that of the old country, these Norwegians found their financial conditions "far superior" here.

After a brief interlude of farming in the southern part of the state, this group invested their meager savings in the purchase of less expensive northern land from the Fox River Company. Over time, almost all of the household heads became independent farmers.

Although one observer thought these newcomers "became early and thoroughly Americanized," he admitted that they retained certain vestiges of their old country.[24] Their churches, denominational schools, and language remained thoroughly Norwegian through at least two generations. They did, however, accept native dress and customs, and they formed no separate institutions other than those mentioned. As a whole, therefore, they appeared rather moderately assimilated.

The most notable among the smaller groups from northern and western Europe were the Swiss, Swedes, and Danes. Although Swiss people scattered over the state and Swiss settlements emerged in Buffalo County on the Mississippi and in Milwaukee, the most prominent Swiss community was New Glarus in Green County.[25] In 1845, a colony of Swiss farmers chose that location as a place to escape from an economic depression at home. They named their village after the canton of their origin and there reconstructed a tightly knit Swiss community. In time, the little burg of some 200 people in 1890 developed into a minor commercial, but a major social, center for the 3,000 Swiss in the county.

The tone of the area was distinctly conservative. The people as late as 1890 spoke German and perpetuated the "gemütlichkeit" culture of their homeland. Dress styles remained noticeably Swiss-influenced and though a public school taught in English, a private one gave instruction in German. Only an Evangelical Association challenged the dominant Reformed Church. New Glarus was, in short, a tiny reproduction of German-speaking Switzerland.

In 1841, O. C. Lange, by his own account the first Swede in Chicago, convinced a small contingent of his countryment to settle in little Pine Lake, 40 miles west of Milwaukee.[26] Wisconsin's major Swedish influx came, however, in the three decades between 1870 and 1900, with the largest number (a net of 12,000 people) arriving in the 1880s. By 1900, Swedes also had become a major element in the farming population of the cold northwestern counties (Douglas, Polk, Burnett, Pierce, Bayfield, Ashland, and Price) and in Marinette.

One Swedish community in these sparsely settled areas consisted of the 50 families in the town of Washburn in Bayfield County.[27] Most of these settlers arrived after 1880, having first lived in other regions of the United States. These newcomers came as individuals or in family groups, paying their own expenses and later sending money home so that others could follow. Regardless of when they arrived, however, they all shared the hope of a better material life on an American homestead.

By 1889, this Swedish community had begun to melt into the broader society of the county. Although the people kept their memberships in the Swedish Lutheran Church, about half of them learned the English language. The children attended public schools. In farming, manners, and dress, these Swedes adopted American ways. Generally, while the first generation held firmly to old world traditions, the second and third moved slowly toward assimilation.

Danish settlement in Wisconsin began with builder and contractor John S. Bang, who came to Racine in 1839 or 1840, and although smaller groups settled in Brown and Polk Counties, the Racine area thereafter boasted the most important concentration of Danes in the state.[28] The Danish-born population of Racine County rose from 1,294 in 1870, the year of the first census giving their figures separately, to a peak of 4,387 in 1920.[29] In 1900, over 2,300 Danes lived in Racine, and in 1905, that city had the highest percentage of Danes of any city outside of Denmark.[30] In a standard joke of the times, a local comedian would ask, "Where was Racine ten years ago?" and receive the reply, "In Denmark."[31]

The Danes of Racine left Europe in hopes of finding prosperity in America. Pushed out of jobs at home by a "too pronounced reproduction of the working class," many of these people felt the lure of Wisconsin through letters from friends and relatives newly-arrived in Racine. In fact, according to one account, Danes annually wrote an average of four letters each to Denmark. One man, Rasmus Sorenson, organized a letter-writing campaign that involved hundreds of Racine's Danes and Danish-Americans and resulted in thousands of American dollars crossing the Atlantic in the form of steamship tickets. Proof of the effectiveness of such letters in recruiting immigrants lies in the fact that one Racine Dane in every three had his passage prepaid in America.[32]

The price of farmland, once as low as $1.25 per acre, and the land's similarity to the terrain of Denmark enticed many homesteaders to Racine County. Even Denmark's Prince Frederick, on a visit to Racine in 1939, noticed the resemblance. He observed that "the rich farmland, the dairy cattle and cozy farmhouses recall to our minds the Danish Islands. . . . The Dane who left his home shores for a wide horizon and new lands found them amid familiar surroundings."[33] A great many Danes, however, came for the express purpose of working at the Mitchell and Fish Brothers' wagon factories or the Case farm implement plant. The Mitchell Company in particular employed Danes almost to the exclusion of other national groups. According to local folklore, thousands of Danes arrived in this country knowing only three words in English: "Vitchell Vagon Vorks."[34]

Within Racine County, a number of Danes settled in three town-ships near Lake Michigan (Raymond, Mt. Pleasant, and Yorkville), but most made their homes in Racine city. They shared the old Fifth Ward on the city's west side with a smaller contingent of Norwegians. This area, known as "Sagetown," also included the factories where many of the immigrants worked, and was a typical middle and working class immigrant neighborhood, built around the first Danish Lutheran Church raised in America. A number of smaller Lutheran churches and two Methodist congregations also grew up within the area. The Lutheran Churches maintained separate schools and from 1900-1912 operated Luther College for the benefit of about 100 students. The two Danish frater-nal organizations, Dania (founded in 1867) and the Danish Brotherhood (organized originally as a veterans' society in 1878), had memberships of 675 and nearly 860 before World War I. Other Danish associations ran a hospital and an old people's home and held many festivals that kept Danish traditions alive in the area.

Although several agencies, notably the public schools and the native and German-dominated city government, urged "American-ization" for the Danes, their assimilation into the broader society came slowly. Their religious and fraternal bonds allowed them room for social activities without mixing with non-Danes; these institutions remained strong for many years. Even today, a Dane can worship in a predominately Danish church, eat his Sunday dinner at the Danish Brotherhood Hall and spend the afternoon with family and friends, conversing all the while in the Danish language.

In addition to the Swiss, Swedes, and Danes, minor groupings of Dutch, Belgians, Finns, and even Icelanders occupied an area stretching from Lake Winnebago to Washington Island off the tip of the Door Peninsula.[35] All of these settlements, however, re-mained quite small.

Largest among the Eastern European groups, the Poles began appearing in Wisconsin at least as early as 1863, but their major influx came much later in the 1890s.[36] The 1890 federal census, the first to distinguish Poles from Germans, Austrians, and Rus-sians, listed only two counties (Milwaukee and Portage) having over 1,000 first-generation Poles. The 1900 federal census, however, showed a major Polish community, with 17,054 foreign-born members, in Milwaukee, largely on the city's south side. Since 15,588 of these were German Poles and since the German population of the city dropped by 5,634 between the two enumerations, it is likely that many Poles had appeared previously in official records as Germans.

By 1920, five significant Polish clusters had developed. The Milwaukee and Kenosha groupings were by far the largest, with over 23,000 and 15,000 Poles residing in those two cities, respectively. Smaller concentrations also developed in the central (Portage, Marathon, and Clark), northeastern (Marinette and Oconto), and northwestern (Douglas) counties of the state.

In Milwaukee, the great majority of the Polish population lived on the city's south side, below the industrial Menominee River Valley. Most of these people worked in the steel mills, machine shops, stockyards, and other factories that extended west along the valley and south along the shoreline of Lake Michigan. As their children came of age, they and their families pushed outward into the blue-collar suburbs of West Allis, West Milwaukee, St. Francis, and Cudahy, all to the west or south. These generations of Polish people organized their social activities around the community's many Catholic Churches, most of them the offspring of St. Stanislaus, the "mother church of the south side." A smaller Polish settlement developed around St. Hedwig's in the northeast section in Milwaukee, near the leather tanneries where many of them worked. There was also one isolated Polish community that had as little to do with religion as possible; this was a fishing village on "Jones Island," a south-side peninsula that juts northward into the Milwaukee Harbor. A rough-and-tumble area of taverns and dangerous night life, this small community was clearly atypical of the city's many working-class Polish neighborhoods.[37]

One of the smaller Polish settlements was in the town of Manitowoc in the county of the same name, north of Milwaukee.[38] Polish adventurers had entered the area at least as early as 1868. By 1885, the community had grown sufficiently to merit parish status and the arrival of its own priest.

These more rural Poles migrated to America to escape the twin economic problems of their homeland: low wages and high taxes. Even though wages included seed grain and the use of a few acres of ground, they remained very low throughout Poland. Few people could afford to own land, but all classes paid the heavy assessments of oppressive governments. It is not surprising, therefore, that despite the difference in cost of living, Polish farmers and farm laborers fared much better in Manitowoc than they had in their native land.

In some ways, these Poles took on the trappings of Americans. Many became United States citizens and participated in politics. Probably a majority renounced Europe's intensive agricultural methods and adopted America's more wasteful, but larger-scale farming techniques. Nonetheless, largely owing to the influence of the Polish Catholic Church, the group maintained its ethnocentricity. The parish and its parochial schools did much to keep alive the language, customs, and manners of the old country. The church, likewise, condemned marriages outside the Catholic Faith.

Although similar to their Eastern European neighbors in language and religion, the Bohemians more closely resembled the Germans in the timing of their migration to Wisconsin. The first Bohemians landed in Milwaukee in 1848; and only two years later, Caledonia, a township just north of Racine, became the first in which this group predominated. More important, every noteworthy Bohemian community had sunk its roots in Wisconsin by 1857, and the in-movement itself crested by the mid-1880s.[39]

Almost from the outset, Bohemians dispersed across the southern third of the state, although they tended to favor border areas to the east and to a lesser extent to the west. Many Bohemians constructed homes along Lake Michigan in Racine, Milwaukee, Manitowoc, and Kewaunee Counties while others journeyed to the riverside counties of Grant, Crawford, Vernon, and La Crosse. The largest Bohemian communities grew in the cities of Milwaukee and Racine, yet by 1920, these included only 4,457 and 1,058 Czechoslovakian-born individuals, respectively.

The Bohemians who settled in Kewaunee County concentrated in the south-central towns and in the city of Kewaunee itself.[40] The earliest settlers arrived in 1855 from Milwaukee, where they had learned of the rich farmlands available farther north.

Although primarily agriculturalists, these original Bohemians became part-time lumbermen as well. They paid their debts and gained clear titles to their lands by "cutting-over" much of the county's extensive timber lands. These people encouraged others to migrate and to obtain properties of their own, by borrowing money or by working in the large sawmills that opened in the city. The resulting population growth continued into the 1870s. Even as late as 1890, Bohemians made up roughly three-sevenths of Kewaunee County's population.

These newcomers brought little capital with them. They carried few personal possessions beyond "the ancestral feather bed."[41] Poverty proved a lesser danger for them than for other newcomers, however, because of the money that, figuratively speaking, grew on the trees of their new lands.

Most of these people had farmed in Bohemia, and they continued to do so here. Some became mechanics and others businessmen and professionals. Nearly all raised their standard of living by moving to America, where farmers and laborers earned considerably higher incomes than in Bohemia. Many kept substantial savings accounts in the three banks of the county.

While perhaps less adapted to American ways by 1890 than many Western immigrants, these Bohemians were notably more like native-stock Americans than the Poles of neighboring Manitowoc County. In farming methods they held to European procedures, but in dress they adopted native fashions completely. As a group, the Bohemians were Catholic, but many reportedly strayed from the faith, leaving the Bohemian church much less influential than its Polish counterpart. Only those who left the church strongly supported public schools, but many in the Bohemian community readily learned to speak the English language. Perhaps there is truth to the argument of the time that the natural bent of these Bohemians was to assimilation, but their geographic isolation in a relatively complete community largely prevented them from reaching this goal.

The waves of immigration carrying the remaining Eastern and Southern European immigrant groups crested in the early years of this century. For example, during the 15-year span from 1905 to 1920, the numbers of Russians, Austrians, Hungarians, and

Italians soared by 264%, 225%, 326%, and 265%, respectively, although part of these increases was due to the redistribution of some Poles and Bohemians under the nationality headings of these groups.[42] As Map 2 shows for Russians and Austrians, these late-comers concentrated in Milwaukee, where they and their children made up a fifth of the city's total population and a quarter of its foreign stock. People from these groups also created several small communities outside Milwaukee. By 1910, for example, Russians resided in Douglas, Kenosha, and Racine Counties; Austrians in Kewaunee, Manitowoc, and Sheboygan; Hungarians in Racine; and Italians in Kenosha and Iron Counties. With the exception of the last-named, all these locales encompassed shoreline cities where the need for laborers and the opportunities for small merchants were great. Some members of other immigrant groups made the trek to Wisconsin, but these groups remained small, and many, such as the Slovenians, eased in and out of larger census categories that often obscured their presence.[43]

One of these more urban groups was the Russian Catholic colony of about 2000 persons living around East Water Street in Milwaukee in 1890.[44] Although the class origin of these ex-soldiers and their families was unusual, their motive for coming to the United States was a familiar one. For their 16 to 20 years of service in the Russian army, the men had received less remuneration than had American slaves. In addition to their daily food rations, they had gained the equivalent of only 83 cents in cash every three months. Every third year, the government had given them a woolen suit of clothes and 20 yards of linen for use as shirts and underwear. The soldiers also received tie-rags for their feet in place of the stockings worn only by the nobility. It is little wonder that they had found such payment inadequate when compared with wages in America.

The experiences of a group of Mennonites spurred the soldiers to leave Russia; when, in 1880, several Mennonite immigrants to the United States returned to Kiev on a visit, their reports of wealth and liberty in America persuaded these men to emigrate.

In that year, 300 families from that city's military community departed for America and settled in Milwaukee. They were so impoverished that few brought anything but the clothes that they wore. As a group, they had little knowledge of money. The meager wages paid to workers in the Kiev area usually took the form of produce and supplies, and much of the region's commerce operated by barter.

Despite some attempts at conformity with American ways, these Russians remained largely separate from other Milwaukeeans. Since few opportunities existed for Orthodox worship, they became Roman Catholics, but this religion still left them outside the Protestant mainstream. A number of them knew a second language, but more often German than English. Moreover, many found the English language, with its several pronunciations of the same letters, inferior to their own phonetic speech. The multi-leveled American government likewise seemed unnecessarily confusing.

They dressed more plainly than did native-stock Americans, and in the eye of a University of Wisconsin researcher, John Roeseler, they were "far less cleanly [sic]." Probably mistaking the restrictions of poverty for ethnic cultural preferences, Roeseler reported that the Russians' homes were "far from being American" because of the scarcity and simplicity of their furnishings.[45]

Roeseler may have echoed local prejudices against these people when he reported that "all of them" made their livings by peddling; that they chose to support large families on paltry wages; that they rarely told the truth; and that "they will resort to all sorts of devices to get one of their fellows out of trouble." Although in Roeseler's opinion they were "not disposed to stir up trouble," they were "very fond of whiskey and other distilled liquors." While certainly a prejudiced view, Roeseler's perspective makes clear that in the judgment of contemporaries, these Russians stood apart from other groups.[46]

Settlement Patterns

Contrary to the early tendency of immigrant group members to band together, as illustrated in the examples presented, by 1880 most of the newcomers had spread across the state and in the process had intermingled with other national-origin groups. At the county level, the integration of these groups with one another and with native-stock Americans was quite remarkable. Table 1.4, which lists indexes of dissimilarity for first generation immigrants, demonstrates the point. The figures represent the percentage of each group's members who would have had to move to counties other than their own to effect a distribution across all the counties of the state that would have paralleled exactly the distribution of the rest of the state's residents.[47] The dissimilarity index ranges from 100.0 (perfect dissimilarity, that is, no group members lived in a county also inhabited by a non-group member) to 0.0 (perfect similarity, that is, group members and non-group members located throughout all counties in equal proportions).

On the assumption that Western immigrants discovered easier paths to assimilation than those found by the Eastern and Southern Europeans, the former logically would have intermixed their

Table 1.4. County-Level Indexes of Dissimilarity
for First-Generation Immigrants in Wisconsin in 1880 and 1920

Groups	1880	1920
British	31.5	22.0
Irish	6.9	18.4
Canadians	38.6[a]	33.5
Germans	28.5[b]	21.5
Norwegians	47.1[c]	46.4
Swedes		56.1
Danes		43.6
Poles	...	44.8
Russians	...	39.7
Czechs	...	35.7
Austrians	...	32.0
Hungarians	...	50.3
Italians	...	53.3

Source: The U.S. Censuses for: 1880 (Washington, 1883), *Compendium,* Table 31, pp. 539-540, and 1920 (Washington, 1922), Vol. III, Table 12, pp. 1135-1136.

[a]This figure is for British Americans, that is, those from British-America (Canada).

[b]This figure is for those from the "German Empire."

[c]This figure is for Scandinavians as a group.

residences with those of other origins more thoroughly than did the latter. However, judging from the 1920 figures, this was not entirely the case. According to Table 1.4, the Irish, Germans and British were least clustered; the Canadians, Austrians, Czechs, and Russians were somewhat less so; the Poles, Danes, and Norwegians formed a third echelon; and Hungarians, Italians, and Swedes were most tightly drawn together. Only for these last three 1920 groups were the indexes over 50%.

Aside from those of the Scandinavians and Canadians, the figures rather clearly separate the Western from Eastern Europeans. The Scandinavian tendency to cluster had various causes. The Norwegian concentrations in the Mississippi River counties represented the rear portion of the larger Norwegian push into Minnesota. The Danish cluster in the city of Racine resulted in part from deliberate recruitment for the wagon and farm implement factories. The comparatively large Swedish population in the northern counties was largely due to those people's desires for farmlands, despite their arrival after the best ground in the more temperate regions had vanished. The relatively high index figure of the Canadians is the result of an unexplainable cluster of 1,880 people in Douglas County that pushed up the Canadians' overall figure.

The contrast between the indexes of the 1880 Western and the 1920 Eastern and Southern Europeans provides one final point of interest. There is great similarity between the 1880 British (31.5) and German (28.5) figures and those of the 1920 Russians (39.7) and Austrians (32.0), who came to Wisconsin much later. Similarly, the combined Scandinavian index figure of 1880 (47.1) is very like the 1920 figures of the more recently arrived Poles (44.8), Hungarians (50.3), and Italians (53.3). The degree of an immigrant group's residential clustering may have depended, therefore, in large measure on its length of major settlement in the United States.[48]

From another geographic perspective, that of rural or urban settlement patterns, there was a notable difference between Western immigrants and those from Eastern Europe. Graph 1.1 illustrates, for example, that the former group often lived on farms and in small villages while the latter, with the exception of

Map 3: Wisconsin Minor Subdivisions Having
Large Immigrant Populations Before 1940

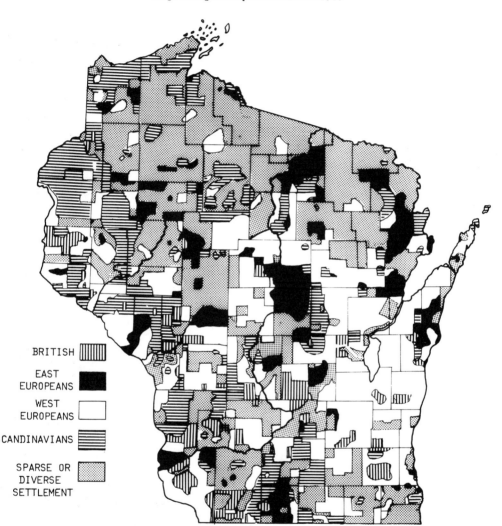

BRITISH

EAST
EUROPEANS

WEST
EUROPEANS

CANDINAVIANS

SPARSE OR
DIVERSE
SETTLEMENT

Note: Sociologists George W. and Ruth Hill drew the original maps used to compile this
single map. Their work, done in the late 1930s, drew data from the 1905 state census
and updated field reports from many areas. This map reproduces the Hills work as it
appeared in the *Milwaukee Journal* (July 4, 1976).

Graph 1.1: Percentages of First-Generation Immigrants Living in Urban Areas of Wisconsin, 1890-1920

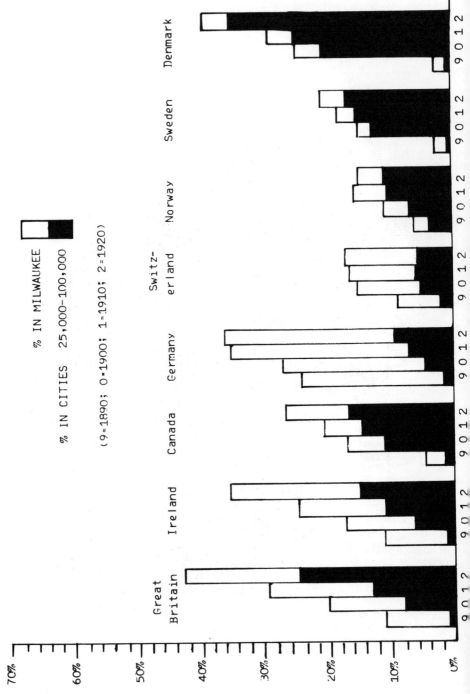

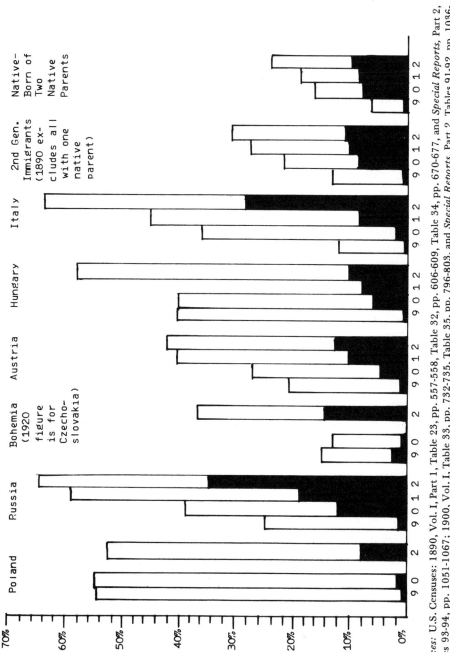

Sources: U.S. Censuses: 1890, Vol. I, Part 1, Table 23, pp. 557-558, Table 32, pp. 606-609, Table 34, pp. 670-677, and Special Reports, Part 2, Tables 93-94, pp. 1051-1067; 1900, Vol. I, Table 33, pp. 782-735, Table 35, pp. 796-803, and Special Reports, Part 2, Tables 91-92, pp. 1036-1050; 1910, Vol. I, Table 35, p. 841, Table 42, p. 191, and Wisconsin, Table I, p. 602, Table II, p. 616; 1920, Vol. II, Table 12, p. 41, Table 16, p. 54; Table 17, pp. 60-74, Table 17, pp. 766-767, Table 19, pp. 769-774, and Table 20, p. 82.

the earlier-arriving Bohemians, tended to make their homes in urban areas. Moreover, the Westerners who opted for urban environments included a substantial small-city component. For example, the Danes of Racine comprised two-thirds of all Danish urbanites in 1910 and three-fifths of the 1920 total. Majorities of the Eastern and Southern European groups, however, lived in the city of Milwaukee.

As a whole, therefore, the Western immigrants covered the state. Yet despite general dispersions, minor clusters of British and Irish persisted across the south while a small number of Canadians emerged in eastern and southwestern counties. The Germans resided in large numbers everywhere except for the far northern and southern counties, while sprinklings of Swiss lived in a few widely separated areas. At the same time, the Scandinavians appeared in several scattered regions. The Norwegians tended toward the south-central and far western counties; the Swedes preferred the northern areas; the Danes chose the southeast. The overall picture of these people is one of considerable integration for those who arrived during the early years and a milder degree of mixture for the Scandinavians. Regardless of their degrees of clustering, however, clear majorities of all the old groups settled and remained in nonurban locales.

By contrast, Eastern and Southern Europeans, who appear to have been less integrated than the British, Irish, and Germans, but as much as or more than the Canadians and Scandinavians, tended to cling to the borders of the state. The only Eastern Europeans to mass in interior areas were the Poles of Portage, Marathon, and Clark Counties. Other Eastern European groups inhabited the western, northern, and eastern edges of the state, locating especially in Milwaukee, Racine, Kenosha, and Douglas Counties. Unlike the Western newcomers, moreover, majorities of Poles, Russians, Hungarians, and Italians resided in urban areas in general and in Milwaukee in particular.

Demographic Characteristics

As noted earlier, the sizes of the native-stock and various immigrant groups varied greatly, but these groups differed as well in other demographic features. In particular, the sex ratios, or the number of men per 100 women, among the first-generation immigrants diverged from those of the native-born.[49] Table 1.5 illustrates that separation.

In the early years of Wisconsin's statehood, its population, like those of other areas on or near the frontier, included a disproportionate number of men who had gone west on their own or ahead of their families.[50] As the state aged, women joined the men and new generations appeared, with this fact reflected in a decline in the sex ratio. While such an explanation largely accounts for the linear changes in the ratios of the native-born, the corresponding curvilinear pattern of the foreign-born figures suggest that another factor was at work.

That second factor was, or course, the substantial increase in the number of immigrants who entered Wisconsin in the late nineteenth and early twentieth centuries. Without question, males led this influx as they had led the earlier waves of immigration. Many of these forerunners were available for marriage and thus are of considerable interest in a study of marital assimilation.[51]

Table 1.6, in conjunction with Table 1.5, suggests the relatively greater extent to which Eastern European males outnumbered their female counterparts. In 1920, the highest sex ratios belonged

Table 1.5. Sex Ratios for Native-Born and
Foreign-Born White in Wisconsin from 1850 to 1920*

Year	Native-Born Whites	Foreign-Born Whites
1850	111	129
1860	107	117
1870	103	115
1880	102	119
1890	102	121
1900	102	126
1910	102	131
1920	102	129

Sources: U. S. Censuses. See note 1.
   *Sex ratios are the number of males per 100 females.

Table 1.6. Sex Ratios of First-Generation
Immigrant Groups in Wisconsin in 1920[a]

Western Immigrants		Eastern European Immigrants	
Origin	Sex Ratio	Origin	Sex Ratio
England	122	Poland	133
Ireland	99	Russia[b]	159
Canada	127	Czechoslovakia	120
Germany	110	Austria	138
Switzerland	155	Hungary	137
Norway	121		
Sweden	147		
Denmark	146		

Source: U.S. Censuses, 1920: Vol. II, *Population,* Table 10,
p. 714.
[a]Sex Ratios are the number of males per 100 families.
[b]Includes Lithuania.

to the latest groups to arrive, Swedes, Danes, and Eastern Europeans, and to the small group of Swiss. Moreover, since the vast
majority of those who settled before 1880 were Western immigrants, a comparison of the earlier figures on Table 1.5 with those
for the 1920 immigrants in Table 1.6 leads to the conclusion that
Eastern European men encountered considerably larger sex
ratios than those known to most Western men. Men dominated
later immigration waves to a greater extent than they had earlier
ones, as evidenced by the high rates of the Swedes and Danes
along with those of the Eastern Europeans. Therefore, while the
sex ratios of nearly all the foreign-born groups stood above those
for native-born, the disproportion of men over women was usually
greater among the Eastern European groups than among the larger
and longer-entrenched Western ones, such as the Germans and
Norwegians.

Although the censuses gave no age distributions for national-
origin groups, samples of grooms and brides drawn from the state
marriage records for 1910 do offer the ages of group members at
first marriage.[52] As recent work on the family life cycle suggests,

the ages of a man and a woman at the time of marriage had significant effects on many aspects of their family life, including the number of children they had and their wealth accumulation over the years.[53] Table 1.7 presents the mean ages at first marriage for selected national-origin groups.

The men of every group proved older when they married than their female counterparts. While the mean ages of the men varied between 24 and 32, the women's means were usually ages 21 to 24. Thus, the differences between the sexes, which probably reflected the men's desires to establish themselves financially before taking wives, was often about three years. For the first-generation Western immigrants, however, the gap was often over four years.

Generally, native-stock Americans and the first-generation Eastern Europeans married at the youngest ages: mid-twenties for the men and early twenties for the women. The second-generation Westerners waited a little longer. The first-generation Western men

Table 1.7. Mean Ages at First Marriage for Grooms
and Brides in Selected National-Origin Groups in Wisconsin in 1910

Origin	Grooms		Brides		
	n*	Mean Age	n*	Mean Age	Difference
First Generation					
Western Immigrants					
Canada	23	32.6	24	27.8	4.8
Germany	140	28.2	202	24.1	4.1
Norway	42	27.5	55	23.4	4.1
Eastern European Immigrants					
Poland	39	25.2	33	24.6	0.6
Russia	41	24.5	31	21.3	3.2
Austria	51	26.7	51	23.1	3.6
Second Generation					
United States	334	25.8	358	22.3	3.5
Western Immigrants					
Canada	36	24.8	38	21.8	3.0
Germany	392	26.0	352	22.5	3.5
Norway	67	27.3	65	24.5	2.8

Source: Wisconsin marriage records (manuscripts), 1910.
    *Unweighted sample sizes.

often postponed matrimony until their late twenties or early thirties, whereas women in the same category wed in their mid to late twenties.

Thus, from a demographic perspective, there were considerable differences between the native, Western, and Eastern European groups. Native-stock Americans clearly outnumbered immigrants from every country, and the Western groups, especially the Germans and Norwegians, tended to be larger than the other immigrant groups until late in the period under study. Among the native stock, men only slightly outnumbered women. The male numerical advantage was greater among some of the Western groups and even larger among the Eastern Europeans, and the Swiss, Swedes, and Danes. Native-stock Americans and first-generation Eastern Europeans, moreover, generally married and started their families at earlier ages than did Western newcomers.

Social Characteristics

The vocational attainments of Wisconsin's immigrants offer some surprises, for they suggest few differences between the two major immigrant groupings. Table 1.8, for example, presents three categories of nonagricultural occupations (columns 1-3) meant to roughly represent high, medium, and low socioeconomic statuses in 1905. The "Laborer" category contains the smallest proportions of most of the Western groups (the Canadians and first-generation Swedes excepted) and the largest percentages of the first-generation Poles, Russians, and Austrians. But the second-generation Poles and both generations of the Bohemians, having settled in America ahead of the other Eastern Europeans, failed to fit the pattern. Contrary to expectations, many Bohemians and second-generation Poles moved into clerking, skilled, and semi-skilled positions. Nor was membership in the upper occupational strata limited to native-stock Americans and Western Immigrants. While only four groups had higher percentages in the upper level than did the native stock Americans, two of those, both generations of Bohemians and the first-generation Russians, were from Eastern Europe. It, therefore, seems only marginally useful to separate the Westerners and the Eastern Europeans when analyzing nonagricultural occupational levels.

In 1905, however, the majority of the household heads of all nationality groups in Wisconsin made their livings by farming. From 74% to 99% of the agriculturalists in each of the national-origin groups owned and operated their own farms. Nonetheless, these substantial percentages allowed room for variances among groups. Surprisingly, the highest figures for farm ownership belonged not to the natives or Westerners, but to the Eastern Europeans. Similarly, the former were less often tenant farmers than the latter. None of the groups, however, included a high percentage of laborers.

Unfortunately, there is a complicating factor in these complicating factor in these comparisons. Higher proportions of Poles, Russians, and Hungarians had to mortgage their properties (note b of Table 1.8). Since presumably the owners of mortgaged farms had less wealth and therefore lower status levels than other owners, these higher rates of mortgaged properties may have partly offset the prestige that accompanied land purchases.[54]

An additional problem plagued both the nonfarm and farm occupational categories. Each included men of all ages and at all stages of the family life cycle. The presence of a number of older, better-established men in one national-origin group could have raised the overall standing of that group even though its younger men had the same status levels as the younger men who comprised greater proportions of other groups. A better comparison of the groups would match their men at the time of marriage. Graph 1.2 offers such a comparison for nonfarm workers in 1910.

Native-stock grooms held notably higher-status positions than those of the immigrant groups. Nearly half of the native-stock grooms listed occupations in the highest levels, and only 11% said they were laborers. Among the Westerners, second-generation men fared almost as well, but the first-generation, with only 19% in the top levels and a quarter of its number as laborers, failed to match the second-generation's standard. Second-generation Eastern Europeans, moreover, held positions comparable to those of the first-generation Westerners, while the first-generation Eastern

Table 1.8. Percentages of Heads of Households of National-Origin Groups in Nonfarm and Farm Occupational Categories in Wisconsin in 1905[a]

	Nonfarm Categories			Total Nonfarm	Farm Categories			Total Farm	Not Classified	Total
	1	2	3		4[b]	5	6			
United States										
2nd G.	29.4	38.3	32.3	11,676	76.3	18.6	5.1	27,958	2,932	42,566
Great Britain										
1st G.	36.8	36.4	26.7	950	85.0	12.8	2.2	2,538	530	4,018
2nd G.	31.2	39.7	29.1	1,634	77.4	20.3	2.3	6,462	410	8,506
Ireland										
1st G.	35.7	36.8	27.5	487	89.7	8.2	2.1	1,559	489	2,535
2nd G.	35.8	36.9	27.3	1,535	86.2	12.1	1.7	7,217	388	9,140
Canada										
1st G.	21.6	39.1	39.3	1,826	90.5	6.4	3.1	3,206	339	5,371
2nd G.	23.3	38.1	38.6	1,075	80.0	15.8	4.1	2,108	150	3,333
Germany										
1st G.	29.1	36.3	34.7	7,742	89.9	8.1	2.0	31,655	3,199	42,596
2nd G.	30.8	45.2	24.0	7,542	83.0	14.7	2.2	27,479	1,254	36,275
Switzerland										
1st G.	14.0	74.9	10.9	613	85.8	10.9	3.2	1,109	82	1,804
2nd G.	42.2	43.1	14.7	102	77.0	20.8	2.2	630	25	757
Norway										
1st G.	25.4	40.6	34.1	2,323	90.3	6.9	2.8	12,227	963	15,513
2nd G.	33.4	45.0	21.6	893	81.7	16.0	2.3	5,152	236	6,285
Sweden										
1st G.	19.8	35.3	44.8	1,372	94.0	4.6	1.4	5,129	279	6,780
2nd G.	25.6	56.1	18.3	82	74.2	21.6	4.2	287	10	379
Denmark										
1st G.	22.1	43.1	34.8	647	86.3	11.7	2.0	3,020	167	3,834
2nd G.	28.2	57.6	14.1	85	77.4	18.8	3.8	345	14	444

Source: "Wisconsin State Census—Studies for 1905," Unpublished study originally entitled, "Ethnic Backgrounds in Wisconsin," under the direction of George Hill, Department of Rural Sociology, University of Wisconsin, 1937-40, SHSW Archives, Madison.

	Nonfarm Categories			Total Nonfarm	Farm Categories			Total Farm	Not Classified	Total
	1	2	3		4[b]	5	6			
Poland										
1st G.	24.3	20.5	55.2	571	95.8	2.7	1.4	3,516	172	4,259
2nd G.	16.9	59.7	23.5	243	87.3	9.9	2.8	537	19	799
Russia										
1st G.	29.8	28.6	41.7	84	87.8	6.1	6.1	181	7	272
2nd G.	...	...	...	...	...	...	...	...	...	...
Bohemia										
1st G.	40.7	31.1	28.2	489	96.2	1.9	1.9	2,462	201	3,152
2nd G.	39.8	45.4	14.9	269	92.8	5.2	2.1	1,021	43	1,333
Austria										
1st G.	15.5	36.4	48.1	239	95.7	2.6	1.7	775	48	1,063
2nd G.	...	...	...	...	89.4	9.4	1.2	85	1	93
Hungary										
1st G.	...	...	...	...	98.8	1.2	0.0	81	8	124
2nd G.	...	...	...	...	...	...	...	...	...	...

[a]The occupational categories are: (1) professionals, proprietors, managers, and officials, (2) clerks, skilled and semiskilled, (3) nonfarm laborers, (4) farm owners, (5) farm tenants, and (6) farm laborers. The figures originate in the manuscripts of the 1905 state census, but were first tabulated into county and sub-county totals by University of Wisconsin sociologists in the 1940s. Owing to the method of tabulation used, the figures presented here disguise a slight undercount of the heads of households of small national-origin groups living in counties having few heads from the same groups. In the earlier data processing, no statewide totals were given. In counties having few heads of a given nationality group, those heads appeared as part of the "other nationalities" figures and thus were lost to any statewide accounting of that specific group. Since the decision as to which groups to omit from separate tabulation varied by county, the inevitable result was a loss of a relatively small number of heads from the totals for the smaller groups. The second-generation figures, moreover, do not include persons from either Lafayette or Langlade County. The given figures for the two counties are identical in every respect, and since one follows the other alphabetically, it seems likely that a clerical error caused the Lafayette numbers to reappear as those for Langlade, or vice versa. Therefore, these figures went into the statewide percentages only once.

[b]Although statistics for mortgaged farms came from a different set of tabulations within the same source and thus suffer doubly from the problem noted above, it is possible to estimate the percentage of owned farms that were free from encumbrance for second-generation natives (54%) and for first-generation and second-generation immigrants as follows: British (68% and 55%) Irish (69% and 55%), Norwegians (56% and 50%), Swedes (64% and 60%), Danes 50% and 47%), Poles (38% and 28%), Russians (first generation: 33%), Bohemians (65% and 62%), Austrians (54% and 45%), and Hungarians (first generation: 34%). The table excludes groups, non-farm and farm, with fewer than 80 members.

Graph 1.2: Proportions of Grooms of Major National-Origin
Groups in Major Nonfarm Occupational Categories: Wisconsin, 1910*

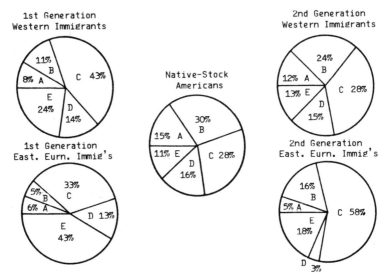

1st Generation
Western Immigrants

Native-Stock
Americans

2nd Generation
Western Immigrants

1st Generation
East. Eurn. Immig's

2nd Generation
East. Eurn. Immig's

Source: Wisconsin marriage records (manuscripts), 1910.

*The occupational categories are as follows: (A) professionals and major proprietors, (B) clerks, semiprofessional, petty proprietors, (C) skilled workers, (D) semiskilled workers, (E) unskilled workers. These categories follow the guidelines set by Stephan Thernstrom in *The Other Bostonians: Poverty and Progress in the American Metropolis, 1880-1970* (Cambridge, Mass., 1973), Appendix B. 289-302.

European immigrants more often fell into the lowest occupational strata.

The occupations of the brides of 1910 are also of interest. Female job titles illustrate the proportions of marriageable women who worked outside their own homes and also give information about the work which they did. From 33% to 40% of the young women in each group listed occupations other than "housework" or "at home." Most of these worked in the homes of others, as domestics and thus fell into the semiskilled category. As for differences among the groups, the Eastern Europeans, the most likely to need outside incomes were not surprisingly also the most likely to become maids.

Of the two criteria (the nonfarm and farm occupations of all males and the nonfarm occupations of males at their time of

Graph 1.3. Proportions of Brides of Major National-Origin
Groups in Major Occupational Categories: Wisconsin, 1910*

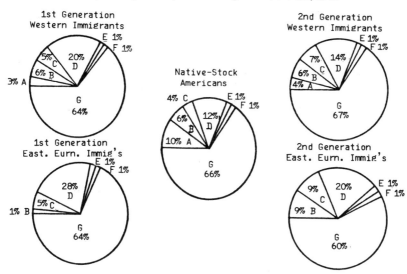

Source: Wisconsin marriage records (manuscripts), 1910.
  *See Graph 1.2 for explanation of categories.

marriage), the comparisons of the nonfarm occupations of grooms
probably is the better measure of group status. By matching men
in the same marriage cohorts, this method separates the major
nativity groups roughly into three status levels. Native-stock Americans and second-generation Western and second-generation
Eastern European ones often had middle-level occupations; and
first-generation Eastern Europeans usually worked at lower-level
jobs. These conclusions are general, however, and a given individual
and his family might have fit at any level, regardless of the nationality background.

In regard to religion, most of the Western groups were Protestant whereas the other immigrant groups were predominately
Catholic, but with a Jewish component, especially among the
Russians.[55] British, Swiss, and Scandinavian newcomers were
heavily Protestant, all but the British overwhelmingly Lutheran.
The Canadians split between Protestantism and Catholicism,
largely along ethnic and geographic lines. Of the first-generation

Canadian immigrants born in the British provinces, roughly two-thirds to three-fourths were Protestants.[56] Germans also were divided in religion along geographic lines. Those from the southern states of Bavaria and Baden, those from Posen, and about half of those from West Prussia and Silesia tended strongly toward Catholicism, with the rest largely Lutheran.[57] Excluding freethinkers and atheists, probably about half of Wisconsin's Germans were Protestants.[58] The great majority of Irish and Eastern European immigrants were Catholic.[59] Jews never represented more than 0.2% of the total religious population. Even if all Jews had had Russian origins, they would have comprised only about 14% of the total Russian population in Wisconsin in 1916.[60]

In the process of describing Wisconsin's immigrant population, this chapter has attempted to evaluate the usefulness of separating Western immigrants from those of Eastern and Southern Europe. The results are mixed, but generally favorable to the division. In several cases, however, qualifying statements are in order. For example, Western immigrant groups experienced their greatest influxes before 1890, and with the exception of the Bohemians, the largest in-movements of the Southern and Eastern Europeans followed thereafter. Based on county-level dissimilarity indexes, moreover, natives of Britain, Ireland, and Germany integrated their residences more thoroughly than did those from Eastern and Southern European origins, but the figures for Canadians and Scandinavians more closely resembled those of the latter grouping. Majorities of all the Western groups inhabited rural areas, while the groups from Eastern and Southern Europe, again excepting the Bohemians, lived in urban areas.[61]

In most cases, the Western groups, usually the largest of the foreign populations, had lower ratios of men and women. Despite this fact, Westerners, especially those of the first-generation, tended to marry later in life than foreign-born Eastern Europeans. In demographic matters, therefore, distinctions did appear between the two sets of immigrants.

Economic and social differences also existed between these major population groupings. In comparisons of nonfarm occupations, especially those of men at the time of their marriages, the Western immigrants more often held higher ranked positions.

Westerners were generally Protestant whereas the Eastern and Southern Europeans were consistently Catholic. The exceptions among the former groups were clearly expected, moreover, and did not challenge the division between the two.

Thus there were important differences in the characteristics of Wisconsin's immigrant groups, differences that often separated the Westerners from the Eastern and Southern Europeans. How those differences, geographic, demographic, and socioeconomic in nature, affected mate selection is the subject of later chapters.[62]

CHAPTER 2

Intermarriage Rates

Assimilation, like beauty, is "in the eye of the beholder." Its definition can be elusive. Note, for example, the case of the Germans of New Holstein in Calumet County, Wisconsin.[1]

In 1848, a group of farm laborers and their families from the area around Kiel, Holstein, decided to emigrate to the United States. Wages at home were low: Men annually earned only 25 to 30 dollars plus their room and board. Women received 15 to 18 dollars, a pair of shoes, and enough homespun linen for a single dress. Thus, when William Ostenfeldt, a Calumet city resident, returned to his native Kiel and placed notices in the local press describing the land and economic opportunities available in Wisconsin, a number of workers readily committed themselves to emigration to the New World.

Aboard ship, these original travelers met several persons from western Schleswig. The latter too sought homes in America, but they were less clear as to their specific destinations. Once they heard the stories about Calumet County, however, they readily joined the Holstein group, and together they journeyed to the Badger state. There, most purchased virgin farm lands east of Lake Winnebago and set about the business of acquiring their American fortunes.

Did these people associate with their American neighbors? Yes, according to the account of County School Superintendent Henry Severin, who wrote that the Germans quickly accepted American ways and, therefore, easily merged with the local "Yankees."[2] The former wore American-styled clothing, adopted native farming methods, and sent their children to the public schools where instruction was primarily in the English language. Although nominally Lutherans, "the great majority [held] very liberal views on religion and [did] not belong to or attend any church." These Germans became solid American patriots, and a full 17 of their number gave their lives in the American Civil War. They readily participated in national and local politics, not by voting as a bloc, but by dividing their party allegiances as did their native-born neighbors. In fact, a "comparatively large number [made] their own ticket by selecting those whom they [deemed] best." Most important, they willingly married outside the German group. They were, in Severin's words, "good Americans."

William H. Fuehr's report on this same group, however, draws a very different picture. By his account, these newcomers and their children remained thoroughly German from their "low German" language, through their peculiar hand-knitted woolen undergarments, to their "German stomachs" filled with "potatoes, pork, pudding [mehlbentel] or dumplings [klösse]." On Sundays, while the "Yankees" observed a quiet Sabbath, "the old [German] folks like[d] to gather in the saloons, talk, discuss politics, or play a game of two of 'Schafskopf,' or 'Skat,' and drink their social glass of beer." Although the public schools did teach English, along with "high German," "Americanization" hardly threatened the community. The German people remained so tightly knit, in fact, that "lawyers would have [had] to go begging for want of clients." Significantly, Fuehr noted that "Intermarriages with other nationalities are not frequent."[3]

The point of this recitation is not the degree of assimilation experienced by the residents of New Holstein, Wisconsin. It is rather that we require a more objective measure of assimilation than is possible from traditional historical sources such as these "eyewitness" accounts. Moreover, for a broader understanding of German assimilation patterns, or, indeed, of the patterns of all imigrant groups, our geographical perspective should be much larger. New Holstein was, after all, one small community.

This chapter, therefore, presents the intermarriage rates of the major immigrant groups in the state of Wisconsin up to about World War I. Throughout the presentation, there will be a major attempt to separate the rates of Western and Eastern European immigrants, to determine whether real differences existed in the behavior patterns of the two groups, and if so to explore the causes, especially those related to such extraneous factors as generational status, time of arrival in America, and metropolitan/nonmetropolitan location. Such objectives promise clear measurements of this important assimilation indicator at a level broad enough to escape the peculiarities of individual communities.

In Wisconsin, a consistent 70-year pattern of increasing exogamy (out-marriage) developed among the first generations of all the Western groups, with the exception of the Canadians, whose out-marriage rates remained high throughout the period from 1850 to 1920[4] (see Graph 2.1). At the midpoint of the last century, the proportions of out-marrying British, Irish, Germans, and Norwegians all hovered below one-third, ranging between 30.5% for the British and only 2.8% for the Norwegians. The rates of all of the groups pushed steadily upward toward twentieth-century peaks (1900 for the British, 1910 for the Irish, and 1920 for the other three nationalities). Even the Swedes (1910-1920) and Danes (1900-1910), whose small numbers prevented their inclusion in Graph 2.1, produced gains over 10-year intervals.[5]

Indeed, departures from the strong trend toward intermarriage were so few that the rates of the British in 1910 and the Germans in 1890 were the only non-Canadian ones that failed to rise above their nationality's own figures for the immediately preceding date.[6] The Canadian percentages appear to have suffered a ceiling effect, in that, having begun so high, they could not increase as rapidly as the rates of other groups. Yet even these figures climbed by nearly half their potential (from 80.2% to 89.3) during the war decade. The lines representing the other four Western countries seem to differ mainly in their 1850 departure points, not in their slopes.

These persistently upward trends in out-marriage are remarkably

Graph 2.1: Out-Marriage Rates for Western Immigrant Groups
by Decennial Years: State of Wisconsin, 1850-1920

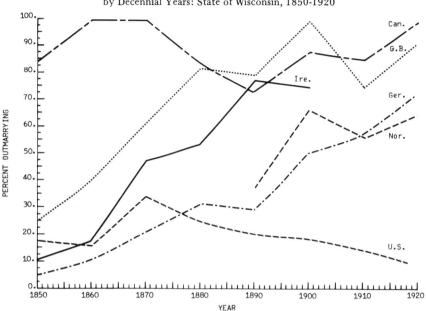

Source: Richard M. Bernard, "The Melting Pot and the Altar: Marital Assimilation in Wisconsin, 1850-1920," Ph.D. thesis, University of Wisconsin, Madison, 1977, Appendix B, Tables 1A-1H.

uniform for both sexes. The only noteworthy differences between the male and female curves, shown on Graphs 2.2 and 2.3, are the smooth rise in German female rates, which is unlike the uneven upward trend of their male counterparts, 1870-1900, and the slight advance in Norwegian female rates, 1900-1910, against a corresponding minor decline in the figure for men.

This charted route toward increasing marital assimilation proved considerably more difficult, however, for the Eastern European immigrants, who appeared in large numbers after 1880. Among these four groups (those shown on Graphs 2.4, 2.5, and 2.6), only the Poles followed the Western tendency toward increased intermarriage. The Russians, Bohemians, and Austrians took a downward road. From approximately even splits between in-marriers and out-marriers, these groups moved toward 1910 lows in out-

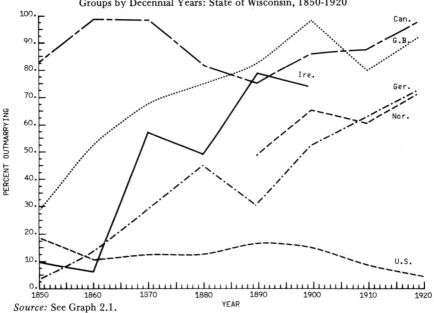

Graph 2.2: Out-Marriage Rates for Male Members of Western Immigrant
Groups by Decennial Years: State of Wisconsin, 1850-1920

Source: See Graph 2.1.

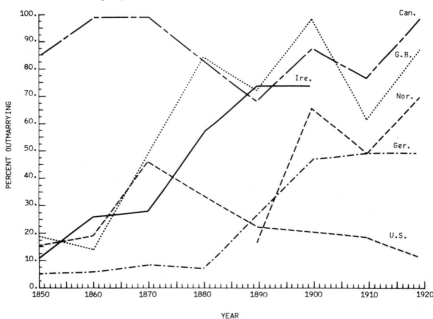

Graph 2.3: Out-Marriage Rates for Female Members of Western Immigrant
Groups by Decennial Years: State of Wisconsin, 1850-1920

Source: See Graph 2.1.

marriage rates, ranging in percentage from the mid-20s (Russians and Austrians) to about 40% (Bohemians). The Austrian decline was very uneven, however, and the out-marriage rates for all four groups rose after 1910; thus there was no observable trend toward endogamy (in marriage). Again few differences are seen between sexes.[7]

At this initial level, two forms of assimilative behavior were apparent. All of the Western groups initiated persistent upward trends toward marital assimilation. The English-speaking groups, in fact, never showed the high endogamy associated with the early days of settlement for all of the other groups. With the exception of the Poles, however, the Eastern Europeans established no corresponding tendencies toward such high levels of out-marriage.

In their specific out-of-group choices, the exogamous members of all of the foreign nationalities were nearly unanimous in their preference for United States-born mates. A small number of ex-

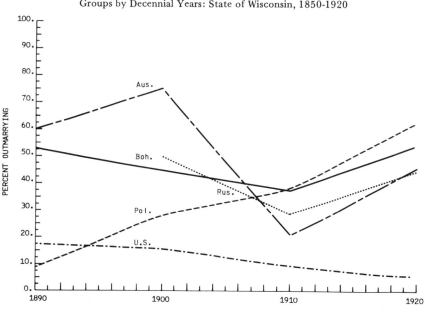

Graph 2.4: Out-Marriage Rates for Eastern-European Immigrant
Groups by Decennial Years: State of Wisconsin, 1850-1920

Source: See Graph 2.1.

Graph 2.5: Out-Marriage Rates for Male Members of Eastern-European Immigrant Groups by Decennial Years: State of Wisconsin, 1890-1020

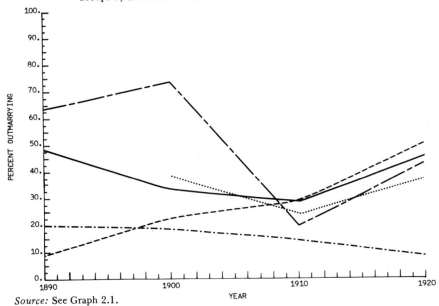

PERCENT OUTMARRYING

YEAR

Source: See Graph 2.1.

Graph 2.6: Out-Marriage Rates for Female Members of Eastern-European Immigrant Groups by Decennial Years: State of Wisconsin, 1890-1920

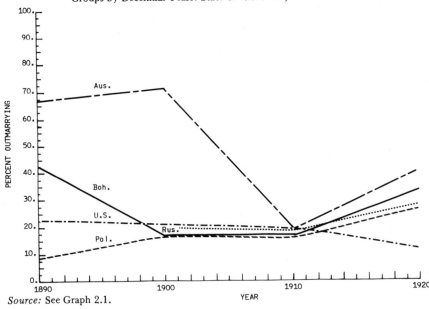

PERCENT OUTMARRYING

YEAR

Source: See Graph 2.1.

ceptions (the selections of Bohemian women in 1890 and Russian women in 1910) did surface among the Eastern-European groups, but even among these peoples, the predominant first choices were native-born Americans.

The second and third choices of the out-marriers are of some interest, although they represent only small fractions of the mates selected. In the early years, the British displayed little interest in non-English-speaking peoples, although in 1850 and 1860, they did marry Germans more often than others outside the Commonwealth. Irish women showed early mixed preferences for British, Canadians, and Germans while Irish men displayed sporadic interest in only one group, the Canadians. For their part, the Canadians alternated loyalties among the Anglo and German groups. The other four Western groups, as well as the Poles, had no outstanding second and third choices beyond a modest interest in Swedish men displayed by Norwegian women (1910) and a similar interest in German women shown by turn-of-the-century Danish men.

Among the other groups, Russians of both sexes showed some preference for Germans in 1910, while a number of Russian men married Austrian and German women in 1920. Bohemian males of 1900 chose a number of German brides. Austrian choices, on the other hand, reflected the diversity once so characteristic of the Austrian empire, marrying in some numbers German women (1900) and men (1900 and 1910), and Hungarian (1910 and 1920) and Russian men (1920).

The overwhelming preference for American mates left little room for other out-marriage partners; therefore, the importance of these other choices is relatively minor. The early tendency of English-speaking people to cling to one another declined by 1900. Similarly, the slight inclination of Eastern Europeans to seek out German spouses (probably owing to language and cultural ties fostered by population migrations within Europe) never reached major proportions. To most first-generation immigrants, marital assimilation meant intermarriage, not with other foreign-born individuals, but with natives of this country.

Despite this decided preference of exogamous immigrants for American-born mates, natives proved more consistently endogamous than any of the foreign groups. After an abbreviated rise in native out-marriage rates, from 1850 (9.1%) to 1870 (23.0%), a slow but steady decline ensued that resulted in a 1920 level of only 6.0%. Part of the reason for this behavior was the preference of United States out-marriers for Anglo and Teutonic partners, coupled with the relative decline of these groups in the Wisconsin population. As the availability of potential British and German spouses lessened over the years, native-born persons had to look elsewhere for mates. Rather than turn to the Eastern European people, they in-married more often.

The foregoing figures, which indicate substantial out-marriage, especially to natives, by some immigrant groups and a major trend toward marital assimilation among the Western groups and the Poles, lend a qualified endorsement to the imagery of America as a "melting pot" of nationalities. The raw summaries, moreover, seem to justify the separation of the more assimilated Western groups from the more introverted Eastern European ones.

These statistics are far from conclusive, however, for they tend to overstate intermarriage percentages by disguising many in-group unions as immigrant-to-native marriages. The 1880 federal census of Wisconsin listed 1,382 Western immigrants who had married within the previous 12 months and who were then living with their spouses. In 589 cases, the spouses were native-born, a fact which suggests a high rate of marital assimilation. The fathers (or mothers in instances where the fathers were native-born) of 386 of these American-born mates were, however, immigrants from the same countries as their new sons- or daughters-in-law. Thus, while 42.6% of Western immigrants selected "American" marriage partners, 65.5% (or 27.9% of the first-generation total) married native-born individuals who were in fact second-generation immigrants from their own nationality groups. Combining the marriages of first-generation immigrants to first-generation and second-generation individuals of the same foreign stock produces an "in-group marriage rate" for all 1880 first-generation Western immigrants of 79.0%—thus denying the claim that large percentages of these groups married outside their own nationalities.

As Table 2.1 shows, this broadly-defined endogamy was particularly high among the Irish, Germans, and Norwegians. Two-thirds of the Irish-to-native-born marriages and three-fourths of the

Table 2.1: First-Generation Intermarriage Rates for National-Origin Groups in Wisconsin in 1880

1st Gen. Groups	1 2nd Gen.: U.S./ Same Group	2 2nd Gen.: U.S./ U.S.	3 2nd Gen.: U.S./ Rest	Spouses 4 1st Gen.: Same Group	5 1st Gen.: Rest of Groups	6 U.S. Total (1, 2, 3)	7 In-Group Total (1+4)	8 Total (1,2, 3,4 +5)
Great Britain								
Males	19 (28.4)*	24 (35.8)	4 (6.0)	15 (22.4)	5 (7.5)	47 (70.1)	34 (50.7)	67 (100.0)
Females	9 (19.6)	6 (13.0)	9 (19.6)	15 (32.6)	7 (15.2)	24 (52.2)	24 (52.2)	46 (100.0)
Both	28 (24.8)	30 (26.5)	13 (11.5)	30 (26.5)	12 (10.6)	71 (62.8)	58 (51.3)	113 (100.0)
Ireland								
Males	16 (38.1)	3 (7.1)	3 (7.1)	15 (35.7)	5 (11.9)	22 (52.4)	31 (73.8)	42 (100.0)
Females	5 (18.5)	3 (11.1)	1 (3.7)	15 (55.6)	3 (11.1)	9 (33.3)	20 (74.1)	27 (100.0)
Both	21 (30.4)	6 (8.7)	4 (5.8)	30 (43.5)	8 (11.6)	31 (44.9)	51 (73.9)	69 (100.0)
Canada								
Males	9 (12.5)	19 (26.4)	19 (26.4)	17 (23.6)	8 (11.1)	47 (65.3)	26 (36.1)	72 (100.0)
Females	5 (9.4)	15 (28.3)	10 (18.9)	17 (32.1)	6 (11.3)	30 (56.6)	22 (41.5)	53 (100.0)
Both	14 (11.2)	34 (27.2)	29 (23.2)	34 (27.2)	14 (11.2)	77 (61.6)	48 (38.4)	125 (100.0)

Table 2.1. *(continued)*

1st Gen. Groups	1 2nd Gen.: U.S./ Same Group	2 2nd Gen.: U.S./ U.S.	3 2nd Gen.: U.S./ Rest	4 1st Gen.: Same Group	5 1st Gen.: Rest of Groups	6 U.S. Total (1,2,+3)	7 In-Group Total (1+4)	8 Total (1,2,3,4,+5)
Germany								
Males	212 (41.7)	23 (4.5)	30 (5.9)	222 (43.7)	21 (4.1)	265 (52.2)	434 (85.4)	508 (100.0)
Females	51 (16.5)	12 (3.9)	6 (1.9)	222 (71.6)	19 (6.1)	69 (22.3)	273 (88.1)	310 (100.0)
Both	263 (32.2)	35 (4.3)	36 (4.4)	444 (52.3)	40 (4.9)	334 (40.8)	707 (86.4)	818 (100.0)
Norway								
Males	44 (31.0)	6 (4.2)	4 (3.8)	84 (59.2)	4 (3.8)	54 (38.0)	128 (90.1)	142 (100.0)
Females	16 (13.9)	3 (2.6)	3 (2.6)	84 (73.0)	9 (7.8)	22 (19.1)	100 (87.0)	115 (100.0)
Both	60 (23.3)	9 (3.5)	7 (2.7)	168 (65.4)	13 (5.1)	76 (29.6)	228 (88.7)	257 (100.1)

Spouses

Source: See Graph 2.1.

*Figures in parentheses are percentages.

German-to-native and Norwegian-to-native matches were actually in-group unions. Only 26.1% of the Irish and 13.6% and 11.3% of the Germans and Norwegians, respectively, married outside their own groups.

Here too, the rates varied remarkably little by sex. The greatest gap between the in-group rates for men and women (Column 7 of Table 2.1) was Canada's 5.4% differential.

Marriage registrations for 1910 reveal similarly high rates of in-group marriages for Western immigrants. Although 754 of 1,352 marriages sampled chose "American" mates, 413 of these people proved to be the children of newcomers who had been born in the same countries as the "out-marrying" immigrants themselves. Thus, over half of those who seemed to have selected natives actually married within their own national-origin groups. A full 65.5% of the Western newcomers married into either the first or the second generation of their own stock.

Only the English-speaking groups had higher out-group than in-group rates. Among the other nationalities, a considerable tendency was shown (strongest among Germans and Norwegians but only somewhat weaker among the newer Western groups, the Swedes and Danes) to continue the endogamous pattern.

Aside from the Swedish figures, the differences between male and female rates again were small. The Swedish gap was largely due to the relatively high percentage of women opting for first-generation mates.

By Western standards, the endogamy rates of the four Eastern European groups proved high.[8] The reason, however, had little to do with marriages to second-generation immigrants, which were few indeed. Instead, the extremely high in-marriage rates with first-generation groups were the prime source of the substantial endogamy displayed by the larger national groups. Of the 704 Eastern European marriers, 582 (82.7%) married within their own groups, but only 68 of these joined with second-generation individuals. Forty-three of these people were Poles. Among the Western groups, only the Norwegians in 1880 experienced similar endogamy patterns owing to very high rates of in-marriages of first-generation-to-first-generation.

As in the earlier instances, little variation occurred between the

Table 2.2. First-Generation Intermarriage Rates for National-Origin Groups in Wisconsin in 1910

				Spouses				
1st Gen. Groups	1 2nd Gen.: U.S./ Same Group	2 2nd Gen.: U.S./ U.S.	3 2nd Gen.: U.S./ Rest	4 1st Gen.: Same Group	5 1st Gen.: Rest of Groups	6 U.S. Total (1, 2, +3)	7 In-Group Total (1+4)	8 Total (1,2, 3,4, +5)
Great Britain								
Males	8 (16.3)*	11 (22.4)	14 (28.6)	11 (22.4)	5 (10.2)	33 (49.0)	19 (38.8)	49 (100.0)
Females	0 (0.0)	12 (42.9)	2 (7.1)	11 (39.3)	3 (10.7)	14 (50.0)	11 (39.3)	28 (100.0)
Both	8 (10.4)	23 (29.9)	16 (20.8)	22 (28.6)	8 (10.4)	47 (61.0)	30 (39.0)	77 (100.0)
Ireland								
Males	4 (23.5)	5 (29.4)	6 (35.3)	0 (0.0)	2 (11.8)	15 (88.2)	4 (23.5)	17 (100.0)
Females	2 (33.3)	3 (50.0)	1 (16.7)	0 (0.0)	0 (0.0)	6 (100.0)	2 (33.3)	6 (100.0)
Both	6 (26.1)	8 (34.8)	7 (30.4)	0 (0.0)	2 (8.7)	21 (91.3)	6 (26.1)	23 (100.0)
Canada								
Males	13 (16.3)	25 (31.3)	24 (30.0)	11 (13.8)	7 (8.8)	62 (77.5)	24 (30.0)	80 (100.0)
Females	1 (3.1)	8 (25.0)	8 (25.0)	11 (34.4)	4 (12.5)	17 (53.1)	12 (37.5)	32 (100.0)
Both	14 (12.5)	33 (29.5)	32 (28.6)	22 (19.6)	11 (9.8)	79 (70.5)	36 (32.1)	112 (100.0)

Source: See Graph 2.1.

*Figures in parentheses are percentages.

Table 2.2. (continued)

	1 2nd Gen.: U.S./ Same Group	2 2nd Gen.: U.S./ U.S.	3 2nd Gen.: U.S./ Rest	Spouses 4 1st Gen.: Same Group	5 1st Gen.: Rest of Groups	6 U.S. Total (1,2, +3)	7 In- Group Total (1+4)	8 Total (1,2, 3,4, +5)
1st Gen. Groups								
Germany								
Males	210 (47.6)	52 (11.8)	27 (6.1)	126 (28.6)	26 (5.9)	289 (65.5)	336 (76.2)	441 (100.0)
Females	93 (31.6)	35 (11.9)	15 (5.1)	126 (42.9)	25 (8.5)	143 (48.6)	219 (74.5)	294 (100.0)
Both	303 (41.2)	87 (11.8)	42 (5.7)	252 (34.3)	51 (6.9)	432 (58.8)	555 (75.5)	735 (100.0)
Norway								
Males	37 (32.5)	8 (7.0)	19 (16.7)	43 (37.7)	7 (6.1)	64 (56.1)	80 (70.2)	114 (100.0)
Females	21 (22.6)	10 (10.8)	4 (4.3)	43 (46.2)	15 (16.1)	35 (37.6)	64 (68.8)	93 (100.0)
Both	58 (28.0)	18 (8.7)	23 (11.1)	86 (41.5)	22 (10.6)	99 (47.8)	144 (69.6)	207 (100.0)
Sweden								
Males	9 (12.9)	5 (7.1)	14 (20.0)	28 (40.0)	14 (20.0)	28 (40.0)	37 (52.9)	70 (100.0)
Females	3 (7.1)	2 (4.8)	5 (11.9)	28 (66.7)	4 (9.5)	10 (23.8)	31 (73.8)	42 (100.0)
Both	12 (10.7)	7 (6.3)	19 (17.0)	56 (50.0)	18 (16.1)	38 (33.9)	68 (60.7)	112 (100.0)

Table 2.2. *(continued)*

Spouses

1st Gen. Groups	1 2nd Gen.: U.S./ Same Group	2 2nd Gen.: U.S./ U.S.	3 2nd Gen.: U.S./ Rest	4 1st Gen.: Same Group	5 1st Gen.: Rest of Groups	6 U.S. Total (1,2 +3)	7 In- Group Total (1+4)	8 Total (1,2 3,4, +5)
Denmark								
Males	9 (18.4)	6 (12.2)	11 (22.4)	17 (34.7)	6 (12.2)	26 (53.1)	26 (53.1)	49 (100.0)
Females	3 (8.1)	5 (13.5)	4 (10.8)	17 (45.9)	8 (21.6)	12 (32.4)	20 (54.1)	37 (100.0)
Both	12 (14.0)	11 (12.8)	15 (17.4)	34 (39.5)	14 (16.3)	38 (44.2)	46 (53.5)	86 (100.0)
Poland								
Males	37 (33.3)	0 (0.0)	7 (6.3)	62 (55.9)	5 (4.5)	44 (39.6)	99 (89.2)	111 (100.0)
Females	6 (7.9)	0 (0.0)	0 (0.0)	62 (81.6)	8 (10.5)	6 (7.9)	68 (89.5)	76 (100.0)
Both	43 (23.0)	0 (0.0)	7 (3.7)	124 (66.3)	13 (7.0)	50 (26.7)	167 (89.3)	187 (100.0)
Russia								
Males	9 (7.7)	5 (4.3)	11 (9.4)	84 (71.8)	8 (6.8)	25 (21.4)	93 (79.5)	117 (100.0)
Females	1 (1.0)	0	3 (3.0)	84 (84.0)	12 (12.0)	4 (4.0)	85 (85.0)	100 (100.0)
Both	10 (4.6)	5 (2.3)	14 (6.5)	168 (77.4)	20 (9.2)	29 (13.4)	178 (82.0)	217 (100.0)

Table 2.2 (continued)

	1 2nd Gen.: U.S./Same Group	2 2nd Gen.: U.S./U.S.	3 2nd Gen.: U.S./Rest	4 1st Gen.: Same Group	5 1st Gen.: Rest of Groups	6 U.S. Total (1,2, +3)	7 In-Group Total (1+4)	8 Total (1,2, 3,4, +5)
1st Gen. Groups				Spouses				
Bohemia								
Males	8 (27.6)	2 (6.9)	4 (13.8)	14 (48.3)	1 (3.4)	14 (48.3)	22 (75.9)	29 (100.0)
Females	1 (5.9)	1 (5.9)	0 (0.0)	14 (82.4)	1 (5.9)	2 (11.8)	15 (88.2)	17 (100.0)
Both	9 (19.6)	3 (6.5)	4 (8.7)	28 (60.9)	2 (4.3)	16 (34.8)	37 (80.4)	46 (100.0)
Austria								
Males	3 (2.3)	6 (4.5)	13 (9.8)	97 (72.9)	14 (10.5)	22 (16.5)	100 (83.5)	133 (100.0)
Females	3 (2.5)	2 (1.7)	3 (2.5)	97 (80.2)	16 (13.2)	8 (6.6)	100 (82.6)	121 (100.0)
Both	6 (2.4)	8 (3.1)	16 (6.3)	194 (76.4)	30 (11.8)	30 (11.8)	200 (78.7)	254 (100.0)

in-group rates of men and women. The Bohemian gap of 12.3% was the only large difference recorded.

The effect of breaking down the United States-born group by parentage, therefore, is to reduce substantially the rates of marital assimilation for all nationality groups. Since the second-generations of the Western groups were much larger than those of the others, the impact of controls for generational effects is much greater on these nationalities. If "out-marriages" refers to all marriages between persons born in different lands, 48.9% of the 1880 Westerners, 65.1% of the 1910 Westerners, but only 26.2% of the 1910 Eastern Europeans out-married. However, defining "out-group marriages" as those that crossed nationality lines, regardless of immigrant generation, causes drastic drops in exogamy rates to 21.0%, 34.5%, and 17.5%, respectively. According to these figures, the Eastern Europeans were still less exogamous than the Western-ers, but the differences between the two groups are much less.[9]

Second-generation immigrants were not, of course, simply pas-sive agents in the process of mate selection. They too developed patterns in their marital choices and sometimes did so with con-siderable independence from their first-generation peers.

Overall, among the 2,008 children of Western-born newcomers who married within the year prior to June 1, 1880, 1,389 (69.2%) chose in-group mates, of whom 984 (49.0% of the 2,008 total) were other second-generation immigrants like themselves. In other words, only about three in ten married outside their own national stocks.

Among those from English-speaking origins, the majority of out-marriers also opted for the second-generation natives (that is, the people of native-stock origins). No other alliances proved par-ticularly noteworthy.

For the sample drawn from the calendar year of 1910, the pro-portion of in-group marriers among the second-generation Western immigrants dropped to 53.4% (2,833 of 5,303), with in-marriages to other members of the second generation representing fully 45.7% (2,426) of the total. Disregarding the Swedish- and Danish-Americans, the tendency of these second-generation immigrants to marry within their national groups declined by 14.4 percentage points whereas the proportion of marriages between second-

Table 2.3. Second-Generation Intermarriage Rates for National-Origine Groups in Wisconsin in 1880

1st Gen. Groups	1 2nd Gen.: U.S./ Same Group	2 2nd Gen.: U.S. U.S.	3 2nd Gen.: U.S./ Rest	Spouses 4 1st Gen.: Same Group	5 1st Gen.: Rest of Groups	6 U.S. Total (1,2, +3)	7 In-Group Total (1+4)	8 Total (1,2, 3,4, +5)
U.S.-Great Britain								
Males	63 (40.4)*	53 (34.0)	24 (15.4)	9 (5.8)	7 (4.5)	140 (89.7)	72 (46.2)	156 (100.0)
Females	63 (29.0)	81 (37.3)	35 (11.1)	19 (8.8)	19 (8.8)	179 (82.5)	82 (33.2)	217 (100.0)
Both	126 (33.8)	134 (35.9)	59 (15.8)	28 (7.5)	26 (7.0)	319 (85.5)	154 (41.3)	373 (100.0)
U.S.-Ireland								
Males	93 (62.8)	20 (13.5)	25 (16.9)	5 (3.4)	5 (3.4)	138 (93.2)	118 (79.7)	148 (100.0)
Females	93 (51.1)	33 (18.1)	25 (13.7)	16	12 (2.7)	151 (83.0)	108 (59.3)	182 (100.0)
Both	186 (56.4)	53 (16.1)	50 (7.6)	21 (6.4)	17 (5.2)	289 (87.6)	226 (68.5)	330 (100.0)
U.S.-Canada								
Males	12 (27.9)	12 (27.9)	12 (27.9)	5 (11.6)	2 (4.7)	36 (83.7)	17 (39.5)	43 (100.0)
Females	12 (19.7)	26 (42.6)	11 (18.0)	9 (14.8)	3 (4.9)	49 (80.3)	21 (34.4)	61 (100.0)
Both	24 (23.1)	38 (36.5)	23 (22.1)	14 (13.5)	5 (4.8)	85 (81.7)	38 (36.5)	104 (100.0)

Source: See Graph 2.1.

*Figures in parentheses are percentages.

Table 2.3. *(continued)*

1st Gen. Groups	1 2nd Gen.: U.S./ Same Group	2 2nd Gen.: U.S./ U.S.	3 2nd Gen.: U.S./ Rest	4 1st Gen.: Same Group	5 1st Gen.: Rest of Groups	6 U.S. Total (1,2, +3)	7 In- Group Total (1+4)	8 Total (1,2, 3,4, +5)
U.S.-Germany								
Males	295 (66.4)	27 (6.1)	54 (12.2)	51 (11.5)	17 (3.8)	376 (84.7)	346 (77.9)	444 (100.0)
Females	295 (47.7)	45 (7.3)	36 (5.8)	212 (34.2)	30 (4.8)	376 (60.7)	507 (81.9)	619 (100.0)
Both	590 (55.5)	72 (6.8)	90 (8.5)	263 (24.7)	47 (4.4)	752 (70.7)	853 (80.2)	1063 (100.0)
U.S.-Norway								
Males	29 (59.2)	2 (4.1)	2 (4.1)	16 (32.7)	0 (0.0)	33 (67.3)	45 (91.8)	49 (100.0)
Females	29 (32.6)	8 (9.0)	3 (3.4)	44 (49.4)	5 (5.6)	40 (44.9)	73 (82.0)	89 (100.0)
Both	58 (42.0)	10 (7.2)	5 (3.6)	60 (43.5)	5 (3.6)	73 (52.9)	118 (85.5)	138 (100.0)

Spouses

generation members lessened by only 1.8 points. This represents a markedly increased preference (from 70.8% to 86.1%) among the in-group marriers for second-generation mates like themselves.

As in the 1880 situation, pluralities (majorities in the cases of German- and British-Americans) of out-group marriers from all groups preferred Americans of native parentage. In addition, all groups, except the Norwegian-Americans, were also interested in Germans or German-Americans.

The 1910 level of in-group marriage for the offspring of Eastern Europeans was 59.5%, a little above the 1910 rate for the children of the Western newcomers (53.4%), but distinctly below that group's 1880 figure (69.2%). As was the case for the other second-generation groups, most in-group marriers (154 of 222) chose companions from the second generation of their own nationality. Thus, the latter proportion roughly equaled that (70.8%) for the second generation of the Western groups 30 years earlier.

In making their choices, children of Eastern European immigrants did not follow precisely the pattern of their counterparts from either Western group. Because Polish-Americans married predominantly within the Polish group, there was room for only a slight preference among their members for Teutonic mates. Americans of Russian, Bohemian, and Austrian parents split their affections three ways: among their own people, native-stock Americans, and those of German stock.

Unlike the circumstances for most first-generation immigrants, the in-group marriage rates of some second-generation groups did differ somewhat by sex. Except for the German-Americans, all 1880 male in-group rates exceeded the corresponding female levels, though the difference between the two Canadian-American rates was quite small. By comparison, among the Western groups in 1910, the endogamy rates for women were higher than those for men everywhere, except among Norwegian-Americans. No clear pattern of sex-related differences appeared among the Eastern Europeans. More Polish-American women married within their own group, but the reverse was the case for Bohemian- and Austrian-Americans, though the differences were rather small.

Clearly, the separation of second-generation immigrants from other natives calls into question the notion of two separate immi-

Table 2.4. Second-Generation Intermarriage Rates for National-Origin Groups in Wisconsin in 1910

			Spouses				
	1 2nd Gen.: U.S./ Same Group	2 2nd Gen.: U.S./ U.S.	3 2nd Gen.: U.S./ Rest	4 1st Gen.: Same Group	5 1st Gen.: Rest of Groups	6 U.S. Total (1,2,+3)	7 In-Group Total (1+4)	8 Total (1,2,3,4,+5)
1st Gen. Groups								
U.S.-Great Britain								
Males	18 (12.0)*	70 (46.7)	57 (38.0)	0 (0.0)	5 (3.3)	144 (96.0)	18 (12.0)	150 (100.0)
Females	18 (12.6)	59 (41.3)	46 (32.2)	8 (5.6)	12 (8.4)	124 (86.7)	26 (18.2)	143 (100.0)
Both	36 (12.3)	129 (44.0)	103 (35.2)	8 (2.7)	17 (5.8)	268 (91.5)	44 (15.0)	293 (100.0)
U.S.-Ireland								
Males	17 (13.9)	48 (39.3)	49 (40.2)	2 (1.6)	6 (4.9)	111 (91.0)	16 (13.1)	122 (100.0)
Females	17 (18.3)	32 (34.4)	34 (36.6)	4 (4.3)	6 (6.4)	80 (86.0)	18 (19.4)	93 (100.0)
Both	34 (15.8)	80 (37.2)	83 (38.6)	6 (2.8)	12 (5.6)	191 (88.8)	34 (15.8)	215 (100.0)
U.S.-Canada								
Males	33 (21.6)	59 (38.6)	59 (38.6)	1 (0.7)	1 (0.7)	120 (78.4)	34 (22.2)	153 (100.0)
Females	33 (16.2)	70 (34.2)	74 (36.2)	13 (6.4)	14 (6.9)	177 (86.8)	46 (22.5)	204 (100.0)
Both	66 (18.5)	129 (36.1)	133 (37.3)	14 (3.9)	15 (4.2)	297 (83.2)	80 (22.4)	357 (100.0)

Source: See Graph 2.1.

*Figures in parentheses are percentages.

Table 2.4. (*continued*)

1st Gen. Groups	1 2nd Gen.: U.S./Same Group	2 2nd Gen.: U.S./U.S.	3 2nd Gen.: U.S./Rest	Spouses 4 1st Gen.: Same Group	5 1st Gen.: Rest of Groups	6 U.S. Total (1,2,+3)	7 In-Group Total (1+4)	8 Total (1,2,3,4,+5)
U.S.-Germany								
Males	991	418	186	93	20	1585	1084	1708
	(58.0)	(24.5)	(10.9)	(5.4)	(1.2)	(92.8)	(63.5)	(100.0)
Females	991	373	224	210	84	1588	1201	1882
	(52.7)	(19.8)	(11.9)	(11.2)	(4.5)	(84.4)	(63.8)	(100.0)
Both	1982	791	410	303	104	3173	2285	3590
	(55.2)	(22.0)	(11.4)	(8.4)	(2.9)	(88.4)	(63.9)	(100.0)
U.S.-Norway								
Males	129	64	54	21	4	247	150	272
	(47.4)	(23.5)	(19.9)	(7.7)	(1.5)	(90.8)	(55.1)	(100.0)
Females	129	65	66	37	13	260	166	310
	(41.6)	(21.0)	(21.3)	(11.9)	(4.2)	(83.9)	(53.5)	(100.0)
Both	258	129	120	58	17	507	316	582
	(44.3)	(22.2)	(20.6)	(10.0)	(2.9)	(87.1)	(54.3)	(100.0)
U.S.-Sweden								
Males	16	13	33	3	0	62	19	65
	(24.6)	(20.0)	(50.8)	(4.6)	(0.0)	(95.4)	(29.2)	(100.0)
Females	16	15	19	9	13	50	25	72
	(22.2)	(20.8)	(26.4)	(12.5)	(18.1)	(69.4)	(34.7)	(100.0)
Both	32	28	52	12	13	112	44	137
	(23.4)	(20.4)	(38.0)	(8.8)	(9.5)	(81.8)	(32.1)	(100.0)

Table 2.4. (*continued*)

1st Gen. Groups	1 2nd Gen.: U.S./Same Group	2 2nd Gen.: U.S./U.S.	3 2nd Gen.: U.S./Rest	Spouses 4 1st Gen.: Same Group	5 1st Gen.: Rest of Groups	6 U.S. Total (1,2,+3)	7 In-Group Total (1+4)	8 Total (1,2,3,4,+5)
U.S.-Denmark								
Males	9 (12.3)	25 (34.2)	34 (46.6)	3 (4.1)	2 (2.7)	68 (93.2)	12 (16.4)	73 (100.0)
Females	9 (16.1)	11 (19.6)	23 (41.1)	9 (16.1)	4 (7.1)	43 (76.8)	18 (32.1)	56 (100.0)
Both	18 (14.0)	36 (27.9)	57 (44.2)	12 (9.3)	6 (4.7)	111 (86.0)	30 (23.3)	129 (100.0)
U.S.-Poland								
Males	44 (77.2)	0 (0.0)	6 (10.5)	6 (10.5)	1 (1.8)	50 (87.7)	50 (87.7)	57 (100.0)
Females	44 (41.9)	6 (0.0)	13 (12.4)	37 (35.2)	5 (4.8)	33 (31.4)	81 (77.1)	105 (100.0)
Both	88 (54.3)	6 (3.7)	19 (11.7)	43 (26.5)	6 (3.7)	83 (51.2)	131 (80.9)	162 (100.0)
U.S.-Russia								
Males	2 (25.0)	0 (0.0)	5 (62.5)	1 (12.5)	0 (0.0)	7 (87.5)	3 (37.5)	8 (100.0)
Females	2 (15.4)	1 (7.7)	1 (7.7)	9 (69.2)	0 (0.0)	4 (30.8)	11 (84.6)	13 (100.0)
Both	4 (19.0)	1 (4.8)	6 (28.6)	10 (47.6)	0 (0.0)	11 (52.4)	14 (66.7)	21 (100.0)

Table 2.4. (*continued*)

1st Gen. Groups	1 2nd Gen.: U.S./Same Group	2 2nd Gen.: U.S./U.S.	3 2nd Gen.: U.S./Rest	4 1st Gen.: Same Group	5 1st Gen.: Rest of Groups	6 U.S. Total (1,2,+3)	7 In-Group Total (1+4)	8 Total (1,2,3,4,+5)
U.S.-Bohemia								
Males	23 (45.1)	8 (15.7)	16 (31.4)	1 (2.0)	3 (5.9)	47 (92.2)	24 (47.1)	51 (100.0)
Females	23 (36.5)	7 (11.1)	21 (33.3)	8 (12.7)	4 (6.3)	51 (81.0)	31 (49.2)	63 (100.0)
Both	46 (40.4)	15 (13.2)	37 (32.5)	9 (7.9)	7 (6.1)	98 (86.0)	55 (48.2)	114 (100.0)
U.S.-Austria								
Males	8 (20.0)	4 (10.0)	22 (55.0)	3 (7.5)	3 (7.5)	34 (85.0)	12 (30.0)	40 (100.0)
Females	8 (23.5)	3 (8.8)	16 (47.1)	3 (8.8)	4 (11.8)	17 (50.0)	11 (32.4)	34 (100.0)
Both	16 (21.6)	7 (9.5)	38 (51.4)	6 (8.1)	7 (9.5)	51 (68.9)	23 (31.1)	74 (100.0)

Spouses

grant assimilation patterns. In fact, a quick review of exogamy rates shatters the simple stereotypes of easy and difficult roads to assimilation for the Western and Eastern European groups. In 1880, the Western Immigrants' exogamy figures for first and second generations were 21.0% and 30.8%, respectively, whereas in 1910, the percentages for the same pair were 34.5% and 46.6%. First- and second-generation Eastern European immigrants in the latter year, however, out-married at rates of 17.5% and 40.5%, respectively.

In examining these figures, one should be careful to note the time factor. A comparison of the groupings in the relatively early days of settlement for each group (1880 for the Western groups and 1910 for the Eastern Europeans) shows only a 3.5% gap between the first generations and nearly a 10% *higher* exogamy rate for the second-generation Eastern European immigrants

Table 2.5. Out-Group Marriage Rates for Native-
Stock Americans and First- and Second-Generation
Immigrants in Wisconsin in 1880 and 1910

National Origins	1880		1910	
	1st Gen.	2nd Gen.	1st Gen.	2nd Gen.
U.S. of U.S. parents	...	29.5	...	49.7
Western immigrants				
Great Britain	48.7	58.7	61.0	83.9
Ireland	26.1	37.3	73.9	81.4
Canada	61.6	63.4	67.9	77.6
Germany	13.7	19.8	24.5	44.7
Norway	11.3	14.5	30.4	45.7
Sweden	...	...	39.2	67.9
Denmark	...	...	46.5	76.7
Eastern European immigrants				
Poland	...	...	10.7	19.1
Russia	...	...	18.0	33.3
Bohemia	...	...	19.6	69.3
Austria	...	...	21.3	70.3
Totals				
Western immigrants	21.0	30.8	34.5	46.6
Eastern European immigrants	...	...	17.5	40.5

Source: U.S. Census, 1880, and Wisconsin marriage registrations (both in manuscripts).

vis-á-vis their 1880 counterparts. Although the Westerners of both 1910 generations married outside their groups more often than did the corresponding Eastern European ones, the differences between the two second generations was only 6.1%.

The relatively high intermarriage rates of the Eastern European groups appear even more startling, in fact, when juxtoposted with the most prominent of the Western nationalities, the non-English-speaking Germans and Norwegians. Among the first-generation immigrants of those groups in 1880, only 13.7% of the former and 11.3% of the latter out-married, as compared with the 17.5% of the Eastern Europeans of 1910. Among the second generations, moreover, only 19.8% and 14.5% of the 1880 German- and Norwegian-Americans, respectively, chose outside mates versus the 40.5% of the Eastern European grouping of 1910 who did the same. When taken together, these contrasts suggest that Eastern Europeans may have assimilated through marriage as easily or even more easily than did many of those from the West.

Up to this point, attention has been focused on the state of Wisconsin as a whole to examine intermarriage on a broad scale. Such a perspective, however, may gloss over important differences between metropolitan and nonmetropolitan localities, for historians and sociologists generally agree that it was Turner's frontier, not Schlesinger's city, that was the crucible for intermarriage.[10] In the case of the Western immigrants, the Wisconsin data strongly support this notion. The situation of the Eastern Europeans is not so clear.[11]

Although for both immigrant groupings, the Milwaukee County exogamy rates fell below their rest-of-state counterparts, the degree of disparity between the two figures proved greater among the Western immigrants of both years than among the 1910 Eastern Europeans. Although the rates of the latter varied little between the two locales, those of the Western immigrants confirm greater out-group marriage in the nonmetropolitan area.[12]

The differences in these metropolitan/nonmetropolitan figures become important with the realization that most Western immigrants did not live in Milwaukee County, whereas, most Eastern Europeans did.[13] Typically, therefore, the Western immigrant was nonmetropolitan and was also the native-born child of immigrant

Graph 2.7. Percentages of Out-Marriers by Immigrant Grouping
and Generation in Wisconsin, Milwaukee County, and
Rest of State, 1880 and 1910

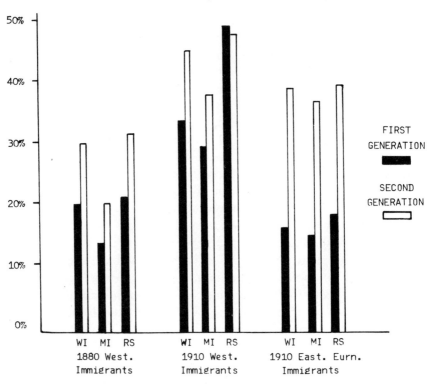

Source: See Graph 2.1.

parents who lived outside of Milwaukee County. With these quali-
fiers, the odds that he or she married someone from another nationality were over 50%, thus, nativists could claim that the
"usual" Western immigrant assimilated rather easily into Anglo
society. The "typical" Eastern European immigrant, on the other
hand, had been born abroad and made his or her home inside
Milwaukee County. Since the odds were low that first-generation
immigrant urbanites would have outmarried, nativists naturally
claimed that Eastern Europeans were less amenable to assimilation.
From such a short sighted perspective, therefore, nativists had no

trouble in convincing many of their peers that the Eastern Europeans, unlike the Western immigrants before them, had failed to "melt." As noted, however, this myopia disappears with the use of the three control factors (generation, time in this country, and metropolitan/nonmetropolitan location) that influence the in-marriage and out-marriage statistics.

In reviewing the various rates of marital assimilation, this chapter has noted initial differences between immigrant groups that seem to justify separating Western and Eastern European newcomers. In any given year, the former appear to be the more assimilative, yet with the application of controls for immigrant generations, time, and locations, those differences shrink to inconsequential levels. To a great extent, the higher intermarriage rates of the Westerners seem attributable to (1) a larger percentage of their groups, than of the Eastern European groups, being native-born, that is, second-generation immigrants; (2) their generally earlier arrival in the United States; and (3) their less urban locations. Each of these factors encouraged the Westerners, more than the other immigrants, to out-marry.[14] Although differences occurred among the assimilation rates of the major groups, they appear to have been more the result of circumstance than of the varying strength of the endogamy norm.

CHAPTER 3

Individual Factors

How can one explain the decision of Peter Christian Beck to marry someone from a nationality group different from his own? Was there something about the man that made him more inclined to out-marry than were other turn-of-the-century Wisconsinites?

Beck, the five-foot, six-inch, blue-eyed son of Thomas and Mary C. Beck, arrived in the United States from his native Denmark in November, 1889.[1] Only 18 years old when he landed, this ambitious young man became a grocer in Racine, Wisconsin, in partnership with another Dane, Jens S. Jensen. Theirs was a small concern and both men lived at the store site (407 Sixth Street). Some seven years after his arrival, Peter Beck applied for and obtained American citizenship.

Eleven blocks from Beck's grocery store, Mayme E. Schruben grew up in a house rented by her parents, James L. and Alvina Schruben.[2] Her father's specific line of work is unclear, but he appeared in several city directories as a "manufacturer." James Schruben had come to this country from Germany; his wife had been born in Ohio and his daughter Mayme in Indiana. Alvina Schruben's parents also immigrated from Germany. After the family settled in Racine, Mayme's duty was simply to remain at home and help her mother with the housework.

On July 31, 1900, Peter Beck, then 29, and Mayme Schruben, 20, married in a civil ceremony. They made their home in a middle-class neighborhood at 1840 Villa Street.

James Brennan was 36 years of age and had good prospects for a successful farming career when he married Clara Hawkins on October 7, 1902.[3] Before his marriage, James had lived in Sauk County, Wisconsin, for many years. Although born in Stamford, Connecticut, his parents brought him as an infant to Baraboo Township in 1867. His Irish-born father and mother, Thomas and Alice Brennan, had not fared well financially in New England so they had taken what little money they had saved and set out for the cheaper farm lands of post-Civil War Wisconsin. There Thomas Brennan prospered and at the time of his death in 1909, "he owned 320 acres of good land, with modern improvements and good buildings."[4]

His son, James, grew up on the family homestead, attended a country school and the Catholic Church in Baraboo, and, in time, became a solid farmer like his father. Although his brother Walter inherited their parents' farm, James was able to secure some 80 acres of his own in the same township, clearing 28 of them himself.

Clara, who had been born in 1876 in Winfield Township in the same county, was the oldest of three Hawkins children. Her parents, Albert and Catherine, were natives of Burlington, Vermont, and New York City, respectively. Both had come to Wisconsin as children. Albert, in fact, was hardly more than 14 when he helped his father clear their farmlands. Like his future son-in-law, he was a farmer, a Catholic, and in politics, a Democrat, having served several years as town board chairman. Clara must have found her home with James Brennan little different than her parents' nearby residence.

Far from rural Sauk County, Adelaide Francis Hickman, or "Addie" as her friends have always called her, was teaching second grade in the Milwaukee suburb of Cudahy when she met August John Scheffler in the fall of 1914.[5] A fiercely loyal native of the Bay View section of Milwaukee's southeast side, Addie was the

22-year old daughter of a Yankee ironworker, John Hickman, and his Welsh wife, Mary. Her father had been born in Maine and her mother in Ebba Vale, Wales.

The Hickmans were hard-working people. John Hickman labored many years as a "heater" in the Bay View Iron Works of the Illinois Steel Company. As a result of her parents' efforts, in fact, Addie became the only girl in her high school graduating class to have the opportunity to attend college. Always the industrious sort, Addie worked hard at her studies and "didn't have much time for running around." Beaux would call at her home on Iron Street, but she never had the time or inclination to become "serious with anyone."

After two years at Milwaukee's state teachers college, Addie Hickman secured a teaching position at Cudahy. Her starting salary was a grand $45 per month, a sum which by her third year had risen to $55.[6]

One fall evening, Addie accepted a girl friend's invitation to a bowling party, where she met the charming August Scheffler. She was struck by his good looks, though she said later that it was his "settled" nature and mature personality that won her over. August was Addie's "girlfriend's father's brother-in-law by his second marriage." As if that were not complicated enough, the couple later discovered that they were distantly related—his cousin was her aunt-by-marriage. Suffice it to say, Addie and August had much in common.

Born in 1877 (and thus Addie's senior by some 15 years), August had returned from service in the Spanish-American War only to find an unhappy situation at home. His mother, who had been a widow for many years, had remarried during the war—much to the disapproval of her son. August rather hastily decided that "things were not the same at home" and, in an ill-considered move, married and started a family of his own. When this marriage failed, August secured a divorce and took custody of his daughter Gladys, who was a girl of 16 by the time August and Addie married.

Although his father had been a farmer, and later a grocer, August was something of an inventor and entrepreneur. Developer of a metal filter used in brewing beer, he moved to Milwaukee in the early "teens" and entered the machine-shop business with his brother-in-law. By the time he married Addie, he was "comfortably situated"—so much so, in fact, that they bought furniture and land for a home and still could afford a honeymoon trip to the east coast.

Only one problem delayed Addie and August's marriage. Addie's mother, like her daughter a devout Methodist, raised a religious objection. She did not care that August was an Evangelical Lutheran, but she strongly objected to the fact that he had been divorced. When August assured the pastor at Bay View Methodist Church that the divorce had been for "the Biblical reason," the pastor and Mrs. Hickman relaxed their opposition. On June 28, 1916, Addie and August became Mr. and Mrs. August Scheffler at a Methodist ceremony in the home of the brides' parents.

A contemporary of Addie Scheffler was Rose Angeline Robakowski, a "working girl," who lived in St. Stanislaus' Parish on the ethnically jumbled south side of Milwaukee.[7] Both her parents had migrated from Poland to that Wisconsin city, where her father found employment as an iron moulder. While his income should have been sufficient for Angeline to remain at home, she and her father had a "falling out." After her mother died, Angeline's father remarried, but unfortunately the daughter and step-mother could not get along. Angeline moved in with some friends in the neighborhood and went to work as a leathercutter in a shoe factory at the end of the block. There she struggled along on her meager wages of 3 to 4 dollars per week.

It was at St. Stanislaus that she met Paul Roman Poczoch (later Paul Pace), a 24-year old fisherman and sailor. Paul, like Angeline who was his junior by some six years, was a native-born Milwaukeean. His parents too were immigrants, but from Germany, not Poland.

Paul's father, who had claimed poor eyesight on his military conscription papers, had fled West Prussia in 1888 in order to avoid induction into the Kaiser's army. Once in Milwaukee, he married and settled down to life as a commercial fisherman. Eventually, he was able to buy his own boat and command a crew of eight men.

From the time of his mother's death when he was eight years

of age, young Paul probably had spent much of his time at his father's side on the choppy waters of Lake Michigan. Later he joined the United States Navy, from which he had just returned when he and Angeline married on May 2, 1917. On the marriage registration form he listed his occupation, somewhat optimistically, as "lake captain." Actually, at the time, he was an unemployed seaman—a fact that makes his father's objection to his marrying a "poor girl" seem a bit ironic.

Each of these four couples married across nationality lines. Peter Beck was Danish, but he married the native-born daughter of a German immigrant. James Brennan, a second-generation Irishman, married a native-stock American. Addie Hickman, herself the daughter of a Welsh mother, wed the son of German immigrants, and Angeline Robakowski and her husband were the children of Polish and German parents, respectively.

Why did these eight people, and thousands of others as well, marry outside their own national-origin groups? Given the uniqueness of each individual's own decision-making, is it possible to pinpoint common characteristics among such out-marriers that may have swayed their thinking? More specifically, what role did the socioeconomic traits of such people play in their selection of outgroup mates?

Over the last 50 years, social scientists have examined the social attributes of exogamous and endogamous individuals in hopes of isolating particular traits associated with intermarriage. Although their works focused on highly diverse settings, groups, and characteristics, these researchers produced findings that might be generalized under two broad headings of causation. The first attributes intermarriage to the effects of an individual's own social make-up, independent of the traits of the people around him or her. The second emphasizes the relationships between an individual, with his or her own characteristics and other marriageable persons (from the original individual's in-group and out-group) and their social attributes.

This chapter examines the first of these possible causes to determine whether out-marriers tended to have certain socioeconomic characteristics that differentiated them from in-marriers. In effect, the chapter tests the applicability of a number of mid-twentieth century theories about the causes of intermarriage to the actual cases of native-stock Americans and Western and Eastern European immigrants in early twentieth-century Wisconsin. The procedure involves a synthesis of the earlier work into an analytical model examining marital assimilation. The central objective then is to test this model through use of Wisconsin marriage data from 1910.

The socioeconomic model of marital assimilation originates in the notion that regardless of the characteristics of available potential mates, people with certain traits were more inclined than others toward intermarriage. In this concept, the individual's decision to marry outside his or her own group was, at least in part, a product of his or her own socioeconomic background.[8]

The four couples identified earlier illustrate many, though not all, of the individual attributes that social scientists have identified with the decision to out-marry. For example, a number of scholars have cited a person's exposure to cultures other than his or her own as a major determinant of exogamy. In work ranging from the early efforts of sociologist Julius Drachsler in 1920 to Milton Barron's most recent book published in 1972, researchers have reported that second-generation immigrants—people such as Mayme Schruben and Angeline Robakowski—were likely candidates for marital assimilation.[9] These individuals spent their formative, childhood years in the United States where they came in contact with people from a number of different backgrounds. Even if they lived in relatively homogeneous villages, or neighborhoods of large cities such as Milwaukee, they probably experienced more cultural diversity in their environments than had their parents when they were young. As the *Racine Journal* later noted:

> [The] tradition of "clannishness" has been fading in the new generation. Slowly the melting pot theory has been taking hold. Danish girls marry Bohemian boys; Irish boys marry German girls; foreign languages give way to English; European customs to American ideas.[10]

The birthplace of an individual's parents provide a second indicator of the degree of cultural variance in his or her background. Perhaps people such as Addie Hickman, whose parents' marriage crossed international lines, were themselves more likely to out-marry. This is one of the conclusions of researchers James Bossard and John L. Thomas.[11]

Sociologist John Burma would have noted that James Brennan and August Scheffler were 36 and 39, respectively, when they married; basing his conclusions on research in Los Angeles from 1948 to 1959, Burma argued that older people tended to inter-marry more often than younger individuals.[12] According to Barron, such a contention is logical if out-marriage served as a last resort against remaining single. Younger people may have waited for acceptable mates to appear within their own groups, but older individuals, such as Brennan and Scheffler, may have felt com-pelled to marry when the opportunity arose, despite nationality differences.[13]

Burma also found that among nonwhites, previously married persons, people like August Scheffler, were more likely to out-marry than were persons entering matrimony for the first time.[14] As in the case of older people, Barron suggested that remarriers proved less concerned about finding in-group mates because they, more than others, faced the alternative of living alone.[15]

Three or perhaps four of the people named were Protestants. Addie Hickman was a Methodist. Her husband was raised as an Evangelical Lutheran. Peter Beck came from Protestant Denmark. Only Mayme Schruben's religion seems unclear, since her ancestors came from Germany, a land with a substantial Catholic minority. One researcher, Drachsler, thought that coming as a Protestant to a predominately Protestant state might have increased the chance of intermarriage across nationality lines.[16]

Although none of the six individuals named could be classified as upper-class in status, some of their well-placed contemporaries may have felt even freer to out-marry. Several social scientists, beginning with Drachsler and including August Hollingshead, have contended that members of the upper classes intermarried more than did other people.[17] These researchers theorized that people with wealth and prestige could more easily become acquainted with other societies and more readily escape the cultural restric-tions of home and workplace.[18]

The ability to speak the English or German language might well have eased assimilation into the major population groups in

Wisconsin. James Brennan provides an example. Being of Irish parents, he doubtless spoke English, an ability that must have made him more likely to meet and marry a native-stock American than a man who spoke only Russian or Polish. Sociologists Niles Carpenter and Paul C. Glick noted the obvious fact that communicating in the same language, if not a prerequisite for courtship, certainly must have facilitated matters.[19] Surely traveler Konrad Bercovici overstated his point about assimilation in Wisconsin when he wrote in 1925:

> "Frequently the father and mother know very little English and have great difficulty in understanding one another. In fact, some of these intermarried people have been compelled to learn the English language as a matter of intercourse, a sort of mutual tongue between them.[20]

Finally, several scholars have considered community size as a social characteristic. In this regard, historians such as John Hawgood and sociologists such as Carpenter have long agreed that intermarriage was more likely in rural areas, such as Baraboo and Winfield Townships where James Brennan and Clara Hawkins lived, than in cities like Milwaukee.[21] By this logic, Peter Beck, as a resident of the small city of Racine, might have been less likely to out-marry than farmer James Brennan, but perhaps more likely to have done so than a Milwaukeean such as Paul Poczoch.

Based on these various sociological theories, the composite model of individual characteristics specifies that individuals with certain attributes tended to out-marry. These included (1) birth in the United States (second-generation status), (2) mixed parentage, (3) greater age, (4) one or more previous marriages, (5) origins in a Protestant country, (6) higher social class, (7) a background among English- or German-speaking peoples, and (8) location in a small community.[22]

Testing the individual-characteristics model of marital assimilation involves examinations of both the effects of the model, taken as a whole, on the decision to out-marry and the relative importance of the specific traits in producing that effect. The procedure used is stepwise multiple regression analysis.[23] Table 3.1 displays the results of this exercise for the native stock and the Western and Eastern European immigrant groupings, since the samples of

Table 3.1. Multiple Regression Coefficients for
Out-Group Marriage and the Components of the
Individual-Characteristics Model in Wisconsin in 1910

	Native Stock		Western Immigrants		East. European Immigrants	
	B	β	B	β	B	β
Independent variables						
Generation	...	...	.169	.149	.171	.185
			(.013)[a]		(.014)	
Parents' marriage	...	...	.183	.172	.392	.261
			(.012)		(.022)	
Age	-.002[b]	-.026[b]	.006	.096	.003	.057
	(.001)		(.001)		(.001)	
Previous marriage	...	...	...	...	.193	.120
					(.027)	
Occupational level						
Upper	...	...	...	...	.533	.112
					(.067)	
Upper-middle	...	...	...	...	.316	.099
					(.045)	
Middle	...	...	.130	.065	.297	.133
			(.021)		(.031)	
Lower-middle	-.295	-.066	...	...	.691[b]	.103[b]
	(.043)				(.095)	
Residence						
Milwaukee	...	...	.234[b]	.146[b]	...	...
			(.018)			
Small city	...	...	.177	.152	...	...
			(.014)			
Small town	...	...	.135	.109	...	...
			(.014)			
Multiple R	.071		.318		.449	
Multiple R^2	.005		.101		.201	
Adjusted R^2	.005		.100		.200	
Standard error	.499		.474		.397	
Constant	.555		-.148		-.119	
Weighted n	11,024		8,063		4,124	
n	685		672		404	

[a](Standard errors of B coefficients in parentheses.) All figures are significant at the .001 level.
[b]Figure in disagreement with the model.

the individual nationality groups were too small for independent regression runs. The table reports the results for the variables that demonstrated the strongest effects on the out-marriage decisions of each of the three.[24]

The magnitude of the multiple correlation coefficients (Multiple Rs) indicate the relationship of the independent variables, that is, the social characteristics of the individuals, to the dependent variable, the decision whether to out-marry. Although social scientists differ over how large this coefficient must be before it is important, it is possible to use the figure to demonstrate the total impact of the independent variables on the dependent one. Squaring the coefficient produces the percentage of the variance in the latter attributable to the independent factors. In this case, the squared coefficients adjusted for sample sizes (Adjusted R^2s) represent the likelihood that, based on the social characteristics in question, one could predict whether an individual had actually out-married or in-married.

Unfortunately, two of the three Adjusted R^2s in Table 3.1 are quite small by most standards. This fact raises serious doubts about the applicability of the model to native-stock Americans and Western immigrants. The mid-twentieth century sociological theories, which formed the basis for the model, therefore, may prove of little help in understanding the out-marriages of these two groups in early twentieth-century Wisconsin.

In the case of the Eastern European immigrants, however, the model proved somewhat more effective. Given the many unexplainable, not to mention unmeasurable, factors involved in mate selection, this grouping's Adjusted R^2 of .200 merits further discussion. If the social characteristics of the members of these groups had that much influence on their out-marriage rates, it seems worthwhile to explore the relative importance of the particular traits involved.

The B and beta coefficients from the regression equation provide this information. They demonstrate the importance of the independent variables to the total impact on the intermarriage decision. The B-coefficients represent the actual effects of the independent variables while the betas, which are B-coefficients adjusted to common units of size, demonstrate the relative value of each characteristic as compared with the others.

The signs of the coefficients indicate the nature of the relationship. If an increase in the value of an independent variable provokes an increase in the value of the dependent variable, the relationship, as illustrated by the sign, is positive. The same is true if a decline in the value of the independent variables causes a corresponding reduction in the dependent variable. If the latter's reaction is in the opposite direction, the relationship is a negative one.

In the case of the Eastern Europeans, these signs provide noteworthy substantiation for earlier theories. The model supplies helpful information about the nature of the relationships between the social traits and the decisions to out-marry.

The most important social attribute promoting out-marriage among Eastern Europeans was mixed parentage. The next was second-generation status. Since these two factors represented the degree of cultural diversity people encountered in childhood, this single concept seems to have been the most important of the traits examined here. These findings suggest that, contrary to Milton Gordon's claim, cultural assimilation may have made a significant contribution to marital assimilation, at least among the Eastern European immigrants living in Wisconsin.[25]

Upper-level occupational positions (such as those held by major proprietors and professionals), upper-middle positions (those of minor proprietors, semiprofessionals, and clerks) and middle-level occupations (skilled trades) all correlated fairly strongly with out-marriage. That the middle-level occupations proved more important to out-marriage than the highest positions may have been owing to continued prejudice in the upper level of native-stock society against Eastern Europeans, regardless of their occupational attainments.

Employment as a semiskilled worker also correlated with out-marriage, however, and this factor was simply not anticipated by the model. Regardless of the reason, these workers proved as likely as major proprietors and professionals to out-marry.

Prior marriage also had a positive effect on out-marriage, as did age. The impact of the latter, however, was quite small. Perhaps there is a grain of truth in the suggestion that previously married people were less inclined to wait for in-group mates, but the corresponding notion about older people proved of relatively little importance in the marital decision.

At the statewide level, therefore, the individual-characteristics model does provide useful insights into the out-marriages of Eastern Europeans, such as Angeline Robakowski. It correctly identifies a number of social factors that encouraged these people to out-marry, the most important being the exposure to other cultures in childhood. At least among the members of this grouping, individual social attributes did play a role in marital assimilation. The model fails, however, to contribute much to our understanding of the decision of native-stock Americans, such as Clara Hawkins, or Western immigrants, represented by the six individuals named earlier, to marry outside their own nationality groups.

These conclusions seem clear for the state of Wisconsin as a whole, but would they prove as valid for a major metropolitan area such as Milwaukee? After all, most of the sociological literature, from which the individual-characteristics model was drawn, focuses on urban areas. Perhaps their particular traits affected urbanites in ways different from the effects of similar characteristics on rural or small town dwellers. Is it possible that a causative model that proved largely inapplicable at the statewide level for native-stock Americans and Western immigrants could, nevertheless, explain much about marital decision-making in an urban environment? Table 3.2, which studies only the city of Milwaukee, offers at least partial answers to these questions.[26]

An initial glance at the Adjusted R^2s of this table suggests that the model's explanatory power for both immigrant groups in Milwaukee is roughly the same as in the state as a whole. For Western immigrants, the Adjusted R^2 in Milwaukee is slightly below the combined state figure (.092 versus .100) and for Eastern Europeans it is slightly above (.214 versus .200). In neither case is the change significant.

In the case of the native-stock Americans, however, the Milwaukee figure (.128) does stand notably above its statewide counterpart (.005), but for several reasons, this higher figure is

Table 3.2. Multiple Regression Coefficients for
Out-Group Marriage and the Components of the
Individual-Characteristics Model in Milwaukee in 1910

	Native Stock		Western Immigrants		East. European Immigrants	
	B	β	B	β	B	β
Independent variables						
Generation	...	...	...	...	.222	.241
					(2.135)	
Parents' marriage	...	...	.325	.264		
			(1.950)[a]			
Age	-8.203[b]	-7.810[b]	...	...		
	(3.505)					
Previous marriage	...	...	.134	9.723	.410	.213
			(2.193)		(4.402)	
Occupational level						
Upper	.331	.154	-.283[b]	-.103[b]	.367	.134
	(7.235)		(4.354)		(6.306)	
Upper-middle	-.336[b]	-.281[b]	...	...	.546	.294
	(4.076)				(4.336)	
Middle	...	...	...	...	.119	.128
					(2.268)	
Lower-middle	.148[b]	.102[b]	...	...	.247[b]	.231[b]
	(4.977)				(2.586)	
Lower	...	...	-.201	-.7990		
			(3.986)			
Multiple R	.364		.305		.466	
Multiple R²	.132		.093		.217	
Adjusted R²	.128		.092		.214	
Standard error	.450		.443		.368	
Constant	.688		.124		.610	
Weighted n	.789		3644		1534	
n	57		364		158	

[a](Standard errors of B coefficients in parentheses) All figures are significant at
the .001 level.
[b]Figure in disagreement with the model.

really none too helpful. The problem is that the B and beta coefficients clearly show that if the model functioned for the native stock, it did so in roughly opposite the way predicted. As footnote (b) in Table 3.2 indicates, three of the four important factors influencing this group do not agree with the model. In effect, they discouraged, not encouraged, out-group marriage. In Milwaukee, as at the statewide level, the model's real value lies in its usefulness to understanding marital assimilation among the Eastern Europeans.

The particular characteristics in the model operated on Eastern Europeans in the Milwaukee area a little differently than they did at the broader level. Here the most important factors were (1) upper-middle class occupation, (2) second-generation status, (3) lower-middle class occupation, and (4) previous marriage. Being the child of mixed parents, the most important factor statewide, proved inconsequential in Milwaukee. Perhaps the most interesting finding is that every occupational group except the lowest and the farmers (the latter being excluded from the regression runs) correlated positively with out-group marriage. Whereas the upper-middle class was the most likely to out-marry, only the lower class among city dwellers did not show any relationship to marital assimilation at all.

The preceding analysis of the effects of individual characteristics on out-marriage relied on the best social indicators available at the statewide level. Unfortunately, the accuracy of some of these variables, particularly those for religion and social status, is open to challenge. For example, that nearly all Norwegians were Protestants and that most Irish were Catholic hardly guaranteed that particular Norwegian or Irish immigrants were Protestant or Catholic. Indeed, those who married across nationality lines may well have been among the small numbers of religious deviants. Assigning religion by nationality and residence, moreover, causes the exclusion of many Germans whose places of settlement were neither clearly Protestant nor Catholic dominated.[27] Similarly, while occupation may constitute a reasonable class indicator for settled, middle-aged men, it may not satisfactorily represent the statuses of young men, often working temporarily at levels lower than those of their fathers, or of women regardless of their ages.

Below the statewide level, somewhat better measures of religion and social status emerge from the linkage of local records sets. Although many such resources still exist in communities across Wisconsin, time and cost prohibit locating individuals from state-wide samples in these numerous data collections. In the single community of Racine, however, it proved feasible to trace the names garnered from the marriage records for 1910 and 1915 in church matrimonial records, city directories, tax assessment rolls, and, in a few cases, naturalization reports.[28] This procedure made possible the clear division of Catholics and non-Catholics and the redefinition of social class by considering fathers' occupations and the ownership and value of parents' homes.[29]

Founded as a trading center by Captain Gilbert Knapp in 1834, Racine had matured by 1910 into a Great Lakes industrial city, specializing in the manufacture of farm implements and baggage.[30] In 1910, the city, located a few miles south of Milwaukee, was a community of 38,000 people, only 8,800 of whom were native-born Americans of native parentage. Nearly 7,500 residents of the city were either first-generation or second-generation Germans, and another 5,700 were either Danish-born or the children of Danish-born parents. The Russians, whose two-generation total exceeded 2,100 comprised the largest of the Eastern European groups.[31]

Intermarriage in the Racine vicinity predated even the founding of the city itself. The first white settler in the area was not Knapp, but Frenchman Jak Jambeau who constructed a trading post in an Indian settlement at Skunk Grove. Little more is written about this man, however, than the 1901 statement of University of Wisconsin researcher A. W. Blackburn. His report, which tells more about the prejudices of his own time than about Jambeau, states that the Frenchman could not be "considered a pioneer because, following the example of so many of his countrymen, he married a squaw and became an Indian."[32]

Tables 3.3 and 3.4, which correspond to the earlier two tables, demonstrate the relationships between individual characteristics and out-marriage in Racine. The data reported there parallel the information in Tables 3.1 and 3.2, except that the Racine charts do not report the B-coefficients. In these tables, the odd-numbered columns present the results of regressions that use the same set of

Table 3.3. Multiple Regression Coefficients for
Out-Group Marriage and the Components of the
Individual-Characteristics Model in Racine in 1910

	Native Stock		Western Immigrants		East. European Immigrants	
	1[a]	2	3	4	5	6
Independent variables						
Generation	...	...	.370	.399	.495	.510
			(.063)[b]	(.061)	(.096)	(.090)
Parents' marriage	.113	.133	...	...	.266	.242
	(.361)	(.351)			(.164)	(.140)
Age	-.017[c]	...	.023	.032	...	.008
	(.013)		(.006)	(.005)		(.065)
Occupational class						
Upper	-.179[c]	...	.099	...	...	...
	(.357)		(.214)			
Upper-middle	.085	...	.103	...	...	...
	(.502)		(.273)			
Middle	-.086	...	.106	...	...	...
	(.138)		(.096)			
Lower	-.128	...	...	...	...	...
	(.497)					
Racine variables						
Religion	...	...	...	...	...	-.079
						(.086)
FC Occupational level						
Upper	...	-.117[c]	...	...	...	.121
		(.492)				(.240)
Upper-middle	...	.057	...	.093	...	...
		(.236)		(.270)		
Middle	...	-.126	...	.086	...	...
		(.251)		(.110)		
Lower	...	...	...	.081[c]	...	...
				(.176)		
FC home ownership	...	...	...	-.079[c]	...	.059
				(.037)		(.065)
PC home value	...	-.151	...	...	...	...
		(.000)				
Multiple R	.277	.287	.440	.455	.578	.635
Multiple R^2	.077	.082	.193	.207	.335	.403
Adjusted R^2	.023	.040	.180	.191	.328	.376
Standard error	.493	.489	.454	.450	.321	.330
Constant	.657	.760	-.182	-.110	-.477	-.572
n	90	90	243	252	97	117

[a]See text for explanation of odd and even-numbered columns. FC=father-child;
  PC=parent-child. See note 29.
[b](Standard errors of B coefficients in parentheses.)
[c]Figure in disagreement with the model.

Table 3.4. Multiple Regression Coefficients for
Out-Group Marriage and the Components of the
Individual-Characteristics Model in Racine in 1915

	Native Stock		Western Immigrants		East. European Immigrants	
	1[a]	2	3	4	5	6
	β	β	β	β	β	β
Independent variables						
Generation	...	...	.297	.273	.261	.333
			(.075)[b]	(.075)	(.087)	(.084)
Parents marriage	...	...	-.081[c]	-.090[c]	.300	.264
			(.081)	(.079)	(.099)	(.094)
Age	.033	.017	.150	.169	.131	.140
	(.010)	(.009)	(.007)	(.006)	(.006)	(.006)
Previous marriage	-.172[c]	-.164[c]	-.120[c]	-.100[c]	...	...
	(.120)	(.252)	(.132)	(.140)		
Occupational level						
Upper	-.036[c]	...	...	...	-.081[c]	...
	(.375)				(.373)	
Upper-middle	-.118[c]	...	.046	...	...	...
	(.503)		(.343)			
Middle	-.032	...	-.095	...	.147	...
	(.150)		(.123)		(.169)	
Lower-middle	.112[c]	...	-.095	...	...	...
	(.358)		(.482)			
Lower	-.094	...	-.013	...	-.074	...
	(.241)		(.166)		(.168)	
Racine variables						
Religion	...	...	...	.070[c]	...	-.096
				(.166)		(.111)
FC occupational level						
Upper	...	.168	...	...	...	...
		(.256)				
Middle	...	-.079	...	...	...	...
		(.165)				
Lower	...	...	...	.108[c]	...	-.173
				(.113)		(.137)
FC home value	...	.112	...	...	...	...
		(.062)				
Multiple R	.247	.275	.321	.321	.489	.532
Multiple R^2	.061	.076	.103	.103	.239	.283
Adjusted R^2	.003	.038	.075	.084	.213	.265
Standard error	.500	.491	.479	.476	.363	.363
Constant	.725	.382	-.027	-.230	-.429	-.372
n	103	103	231	234	152	164

[a]See text for explanation of odd and even-numbered columns. FC=father-child.
[b](Standard errors of B coefficients in parentheses.)
[c]Figure in disagreement with the model.

variables as used in the statewide models. The even-numbered columns represent corresponding runs that employ many of the same variables but substitute new indicators for religion, occupation, and home ownership and value.

As illustrated by the larger Adjusted R^2s of Tables 3.3 and 3.4, the individual characteristics of Racine's Western and Eastern European immigrants played larger roles in their out- (and in-) marriage decisions than did the same traits for either the state's immigrants in general or Milwaukee's in particular. Among the native-stock Americans, Racine's figure is much higher than the state's, but a little below the questionable mark for Milwaukee. Excluding this last figure from further comparisons, every Adjusted R^2 in the Racine charts is larger than its corresponding figure in Tables 3.1 and 3.2

Circumstances peculiar to that city caused higher Adjusted R^2s there than at the statewide level, even with the employment (Columns 1, 3, and 5) of the same variables used previously. This was true for all three nativity groups. For Racine's Eastern European immigrants, however, the inclusion of the newly defined variables for religion, occupational level, and home ownership results in additional increases in the Adjusted R^2s. This latter effect hints that such factors may have been more important, at least to Eastern Europeans, than the statewide and Milwaukee analyses implied.

The Adjusted R^2s of the Western immigrants of 1910 and of the Eastern Europeans of both 1910 and 1915 are sufficiently high to merit comments on the relative value of the social characteristics of each, as represented by the beta coefficients. With the new variables included in the analysis (Columns 4 and 6 of Table 3.3 and Column 6 of Table 3.4), the most important attribute encouraging immigrants to out-marry in Racine, as in the rest of the state, was second-generation status. Among the Westerners of 1910, upper-middle and middle occupational levels (as newly defined) were next in their contributions to the Adjusted R^2, followed by lower occupational level and home ownership. Unfortunately, these last two factors had the opposite effect on out-marriage from that predicted by the model, thus negating the expected linkage between marital assimilation and higher social status. Age was the least important among the factors listed. Over-all, therefore, the social characteristic having the strongest, most positive impact on out-marriage among Racine's Western immigrants was birth, and presumably childhood, in the United States.

Among Racine's Eastern European immigrants of 1910 and 1915, as among those across the state in 1910, mixed percentage was the second most important individual characteristic encouraging out-marriage. This attribute, along with second-generation status, contributed far more to the explanation of exogamy than did the other factors. Next in importance for the 1910 group were the newly defined indicators for upper occupational status, Catholic religion, and home ownership, with only Catholicism having a negative effect. Age was of least importance. Among the 1915 Eastern Europeans, however, the negative effect of lower occupational status proves third in importance, followed by age and Catholicism, the latter again, a negative influence. Among the Eastern European immigrants of both years, however, every individual trait correlated with out-marriage in the manner predicted by the model.

In Racine, therefore, individual characteristics had greater influence over out-marriage and in-marriage than they did statewide and in Milwaukee. This finding partly resulted from unknown circumstances that caused the original, statewide variables to develop stronger relationships to out-marriage in that small city than across the state in general or in the metropolitan area. This stronger relationship is particularly apparent in the case of second- generation status. However, some of the differences in the effects of individual characteristics at the two levels were due to better identification of religious preference and social status in Racine.

The Racine data raise suspicions that these latter factors may have carried somewhat greater importance than suggested by the statewide and Milwaukee analyses. Protestantism (or at least non-Catholicism) and higher social status may, indeed, have encouraged immigrants to out-marry, though not as strongly as did second-generation status and mixed parentage.

Whether their social characteristics encouraged the Becks, Brennans, Schefflers, or Poczochs in particular to out-marry remains a moot point, but it is clear that such factors did influence people like them. At both statewide and Milwaukee levels, this held true for Eastern Europeans, such as Angeline Robakowski, though admittedly much less so for native-stock Americans, such as Clara Hawkins, and Western immigrants, as represented by the others. In the state as a whole, Eastern Europeans were most likely to out-marry if their parents had done so, if they themselves had been born in the United States, and if in terms of occupation, they were middle-class. In Milwaukee in particular, however, the likelihood was highest when the Eastern Europeans in question were above society's lowest level, of second-generation status, and had been married previously. Finally, the possibility remains that religion and social status may have been of greater importance than it was possible to determine from this analysis. Nevertheless, it is clear that, depending on their social characteristics, some individuals were more likely to marry outside their own groups.

CHAPTER *4*

Group Factors

Just as "marriage is a two-way street," there is rarely a one-lane avenue to mate selection. Individuals do not normally choose mates without regard to the marriageable persons around them. Assuming that this is equally true for in-group and out-group marriages, the marital assimilation process must have been at least two-dimensional. Not only must a person have been willing to out-marry—something that depended in part on his or her own social characteristics—but he or she also must have found a suitable prospective mate. The likelihood of marital assimilation, therefore, must have depended to some extent on the relative availability and desirability of potential out-group mates. This chapter examines that proposition.

"Availability" is the key word. Obviously, no single individual could have known all of the marriageable members of the opposite sex who lived in Wisconsin.[1] There must have been some geographic limits within which most people met, courted, and wed. Such spatial boundaries, in effect, must have created "marriage markets," specific areas within which the majority "shopped" for their mates.[2] This fact is particularly important to understanding the effects of group factors on marital assimilation. Just how many possible in-group and out-group mates were available to a particular person depended, not on the total number in the state, but on the total within a given proximity to him or her. Those available at farther distances were likely unknown or of little interest. Similarly, it was probably the characteristics of those possible mates nearby that determined relative desirability. Those of people who lived farther away were likely irrelevant in the mate selection process. Thus, the analysis begins with a working definition of the concept of "marriage markets."

Marriage Markets

Franny Morawetz and Joseph Mrkvicka lived in houses that stood side by side on Douglas Avenue in Racine, Wisconsin. At the turn of the century, the 24-year old, Wisconsin-born Franny, the daughter of German immigrants, was a clerk in her mother's grocery and dry goods store. Her family had for several years lived at the site of this business, 1234 Douglas, adjacent to a saloon that Joseph Morawetz, her father, had run at No. 1232. After Mr. Morawetz died at age 69 in the winter of 1897, his widow and daughters continued to operate the grocery and dry good concern, but they decided to sell the liquor dispensary to Frank Mrkvicka, a Bohemian immigrant who had for some time operated a competing establishment on Racine's Main Street. The Morawetzes, however, preferred to live in the building that housed the tavern, and so they offered their former quarters to the new saloonkeeper and his son Joseph. Since Franny Morawetz lived at the saloon site but clerked in her mother's store at the same time that 22-year old Joseph Mrkvicka lived at the store site but kept the books at his father's saloon, the two literally crossed paths on a daily basis until June 12, 1900, when they wed. Frank Mrkvicka, in short, married the proverbial "girl next door."[3]

Marital opportunity was not even that far away for another pair of Racine residents. Regardless of just where the Reverend C. H. Jensen, pastor of that city's Emmaus Lutheran Church, performed the actual ceremony, Jenny Thorgersen's wedding was an "in-house" activity. Some years earlier, Jenny, along with her father and mother, Christoffer and Moren Thorgersen, had migrated from their native Denmark to their new home in the United States. Pursuing their American dream, the Thorgersens had purchased a modest home on Racine's south side. Unfortunately, the young couple discovered that it was impossible to keep up their mortgage payments on their income alone. Christoffer Thorgersen brought home only the wages of a common, though apparently thrifty, laborer, and, even with the additional money that his daughter was able to earn as a seamstress, this sum proved insufficient for paying the bills. Within some five years of their arrival in Wisconsin, therefore, the Thorgersens decided to take in a boarder. The young man they chose was a 23-year old tailor, Victor Christensen, who had recently arrived from their homeland. Thus, as circumstances quickly proved, at the very time when Jenny Thorgersen was ready for marriage, opportunity rather literally knocked at her door in the person of Christensen. The two became husband and wife on the first day of August, 1900.[4]

Few young people found their mates so close to home as did Jenny Thorgersen. Yet, in a sense, a majority of all early-twentieth century Wisconsinites, regardless of sex or national-origin group, followed the example of Joseph Mrkvicka and married the "girl [or boy] next door." Over half of the members of each of the major nationality groups that settled the Badger state found their marriage partners within their own towns, villages, and cities. In fact, as Table 4.1 demonstrates, three-quarters of both sexes of each major nativity group married persons who lived within twenty-five miles of their own homes. These figures ranged from a low of 76.6% for native-stock grooms to a high of 88.5% for Eastern European brides.

Table 4.2 illustrates much the same point but locates the spouses within specific governmental units. Among those marriers who themselves lived in Wisconsin, roughly half to three-quarters found that the one and only boy (or girl) in the world for them happened to live within their own home towns, villages, or cities. From nearly three-quarters to fully 90% of all these individuals met and married someone who lived in the same county. Again, the Eastern European immigrants were the most provincial in their mate selections, but the rates were high for all groups.

Table 4.1. Percentages of All Brides and Grooms Who Selected Mates
Residing at Given Distances by Nationality Groups in Wisconsin in 1910

	0-25 Miles			26-200+ Miles					
	Same MCD*	Other MCD*	Total	26-50	51-75	76-100	101-150	151-200	Over 200
Grooms									
All	62.0	20.6	82.6	2.6	2.3	2.2	2.5	1.4	6.4
Native stock	53.0	23.6	76.6	2.9	3.8	2.7	3.7	3.3	7.1
Western immigrants	64.0	19.9	83.9	2.2	2.0	1.8	2.3	1.1	6.7
Eastern European immigrants	69.5	18.2	87.7	3.5	0.6	3.1	0.9	0.0	4.3
Brides									
All	62.0	20.6	82.6	2.6	3.3	2.2	2.5	1.4	6.4
Native stock	56.7	23.7	80.0	3.0	1.8	2.8	1.9	3.4	6.7
Western immigrants	62.6	19.7	82.3	2.5	2.9	1.8	3.3	0.7	6.6
Eastern European immigrants	71.3	17.2	88.5	2.0	1.0	2.3	0.6	0.0	5.4

Source: Wisconsin marriage records (manuscripts), 1910.
*Minor Civil Division, i.e., town, village, or city.

Table 4.2. Percentages of Wisconsin Residents Who Selected Mates from Given Geographic Areas By National-Origin Groups in Wisconsin in 1910

	Same Country			Wisconsin			Out-of-State		
	Same MCD*	Other MCD*	Total	Adjacent County	Non-adjacent County	Total	Adjacent State	Non-adjacent Area	Total
Grooms									
All	63.9	18.8	82.7	7.6	7.3	14.9	1.6	0.8	2.4
Native stock	57.1	18.3	83.3	7.9	8.5	16.4	2.0	1.3	3.3
Western immigrants	65.0	18.3	83.3	7.0	7.3	14.3	1.6	0.7	2.1
Eastern European immigrants	75.6	11.7	87.3	4.3	6.3	10.6	1.7	0.4	2.1
Brides									
All	63.9	18.8	82.7	7.6	7.3	14.9	1.6	0.8	2.4
Native stock	49.7	23.5	73.2	9.7	7.3	17.0	5.1	4.8	9.9
Western immigrants	62.1	15.9	78.0	7.2	7.2	14.4	4.3	3.3	7.6
Eastern European immigrants	76.3	13.8	90.1	3.5	5.9	9.4	1.7	3.5	5.2

Source: Wisconsin marriage records (manuscripts), 1910.
Note: The initial columns of Tables 4.1 and 4.2 differ slightly because Table 4.1 includes all marriers, but Table 4.2 counts only Wisconsin residents.
*Minor Civil Division, i.e., town, village, or city.

Clearly, the place to examine the relationships between an individual's decision to out-marry and the in-group and out-group mates available is the local marriage market. The county, moreover, seems the most reasonable geographic area for approximating markets for the vast majority of marriers. What then were the choices afforded Wisconsin's would-be brides and grooms as they surveyed their own individual county marriage markets?

Demographic Factors

At its simplest level, the availability of prospective in-group and out-group mates in given county marriage markets is a function of group sizes and sex ratios. On the group size issue in particular, membership in an especially large group may enhance the opportunities for endogamy, just as membership in a small one may reduce those chances. Conversely, a relatively large out-group may increase the chances of out-marriage while a smaller one may decrease them.[5] From a demographic standpoint, the problem is one of basic mathematics, as sociologist Paul H. Besanceney explained:

> The smaller the group relative to the total population, the faster its [out-marriage] rate goes up with each intermarriage; it can quickly reach a real upper limit of a 100% intermarriage rate. A majority group, on the other hand, will find not only that its intermarriage rate will go up more slowly, but that it can never reach a real limit of 100% simply because there are not enough mates available outside its group. Therefore, to compare marriage rates without this fact in mind is misleading.[6]

The sex ratio, the number of males per 100 families, can be equally troublesome. If the sex ratio of a person's own group favors his or her own sex, that is, if the person's own sex is in the minority, the opportunities for in-group marriage are greater than they would otherwise be. Similarly, an unfavorable sex ratio for the person's out-group may encourage marriage within the in-group while unfavorable in-group and favorable out-group ratios should both encourage out-marriage.[7] Fortunately, by means of the statistical tool of iterative rescaling it is possible to ferret out and analyze the influence of these two demographic factors on out-marriage rates in such local marriage markets as Milwaukee and Racine.[8]

The net effect of applying iterative rescaling to a set of actual in-marriage and out-marriage percentages (Table 4.3) is to create an idealized table (Table 4.4) free from the pressures of group-size variations and sex ratio imbalances. In such a table the opportunities for in-group and out-group matches are equal and, in Table 4.4 in particular, so are the chances of in-marriage with a member of either the first or second generation. In this case, each native-stock American and each immigrant would have had 50 out-group and 50 in-group mates from which to choose and each immigrant would have had equal opportunities (25-25) for matrimony with someone from either generation of his own group. A comparison of the out-marrying figures of the two tables then demonstrates the impact of group sizes and sex ratios on the mate selections of Milwaukee's native-stock Americans, Germans, and Poles.[9]

With reference to the actual percentages, only among the native-stock Americans did a majority of grooms and brides wed outside their own groups. The out-marriage figures of the two immigrant groups, on the other hand, were rather low, ranging between 8% and 35%. In general, second-generation immigrants were more exogamous than first; Polish people were less inclined to out-marry than others; and, surprisingly, females were a little more likely to find out-group mates than were males.

If, however, everyone had had equal opportunities for in-group and out-group marriages, the figures would have been somewhat different. With the exception of the largest group, the second-generation German men and women, all of the groups would have been more introverted in their choices. This is especially true of the native-stock. Although in fact over half of these men and women out-married, fewer than a third would have done so under standardized conditions, probably because of the proportionally larger number of potential in-group spouses who would have become available. Similarly, increased opportunities for in-marriage would have tempted first-generation Germans and first- and second-generation Poles—though for these latter groups the

Table 4.3. Actual Percentages of In-Group and Out-Group Marriers for Selected Groups by Sex and Generation in Milwaukee in 1910

	In-Marriers		Out-	Total	
	with 1st. Gen.	with 2nd Gen.	Marriers	%	Number
Males					
Native Stock		47	53	100	273
Germans:					
1st Gen.	36	45	19	100	169
2nd Gen.	8	62	30	100	418
Poles:					
1st Gen.	65	27	8	100	71
2nd Gen.	9.5	81	9.5	100	21
Females					
Native Stock		46	54	100	278
Germans:					
1st Gen.	51	29	20	100	120
2nd Gen.	15	50	35	100	519
Poles:					
1st Gen.	88	4	8	100	52
2nd Gen.	39	35	26	100	49

Source: Wisconsin marriage records (manuscripts), 1910.
Note: Percentages rounded to conform to marginal totals.

Table 4.4. Adjusted Percentages of In-Group and Out-Group Marriers for Selected Groups by Sex and Generation in Milwaukee in 1910

	In-Marriage		Out-	Total
	with 1st Gen.	with 2nd Gen.	Marriage(%)	(%)
Males				
Native-stock		70	30	100
Germans:				
1st Gen.	60	22	18	100
2nd Gen.	19	43	38	100
Polish:				
1st Gen.	79	17	4	100
2nd Gen.	17	77	6	100
Females				
Native-stock		70	30	100
Germans:				
1st Gen.	60	22	18	100
2nd Gen.	20	43	37	100
Polish:				
1st Gen.	79	17	4	100
2nd Gen.	17	77	6	100

Note: Figures rounded to conform to marginal tables.

findings are less firm owing to smaller sample sizes. The limitations of group sizes and sex ratios thus pressured a number of these people to out-marry who would not have done so otherwise.

Among Milwaukee's second-generation Germans, the situation is just the reverse. Because of the large size of the German group, standardization, in effect, causes relative reductions in the number of in-group choices and increases in out-group ones. If equal opportunities had been available for in-marriage and out-marriage, more of these people would have taken the latter option. Thus, demographic constraints resulted in fewer out-marriages.

The relationships among the subgroups, incidentally, did not change with standardization. Persons of native stock still would have been the most likely to out-marry and the Polish subgroups the least likely. First-generation immigrants still would have been less likely than second to choose exogamous mates.[10]

In the smaller community of Racine, the standardization process, as demonstrated in Tables 4.5 and 4.6, has a generally depressing effect on the out-marriage percentages. Although here Danes replaced Poles among the largest population groups, adjusted figures remain about as low as they were for most Milwaukee groups.[11] This decline from actual to adjusted figures is apparent for all of the subgroups except the first-generation German men and the second-generation Danish women. As in Milwaukee, the drop is the greatest among the native stock of both sexes. In the case of the smaller city, however, there is no clear-cut relationship between group size and its effects on the out-marriage figures. Group sizes and sex ratios are forcing most subgroups into greater exogamy than there would have been otherwise. The specific effects, however, are just not as predictable here as they were in Milwaukee.

In Milwaukee and Racine, and one suspects in other Wisconsin communities, varying groups sizes and sex ratios did affect the opportunities for in-group and out-group marriage. In the absence of other factors, these influences sometimes became rather important, as in the cases of the native-stock Americans. But such demographic factors did not operate in a vacuum. Availability, the physical presence of potential mates, represents only one kind of group factor. The other, desirability, refers to the attractiveness

Table 4.5. Actual Percentages of In-Group and Out-Group
Marriers for Selected Groups by Sex and
Generation in Racine in 1910

	In-Marriage (%)		Out-	
	with 1st Gen.	with 2nd Gen.	Marriage(%)	Total %
Males				
Native stock	43		57	100	44
Germans:				
1st Gen.	22	33	44	100	9
2nd Gen.	17	82	1	100	17
Danes:				
1st Gen.	69	17	14	100	29
2nd Gen.	0	19	81	100	16
Females				
Native stock	40		60	100	47
Germans:				
1st Gen.	22	33	44	100	9
2nd Gen.	1	35	57	100	40
Danes:				
1st Gen.	80	0	20	100	25
2nd Gen.	21	12	67	100	24

Note: Percentages rounded to conform to marginal tables.

Table 4.6. Adjusted Percentages of In-Group and Out-Group
Marriers for Selected Groups by Sex and
Generation in Racine in 1910

	In-Marriage (%)		Out-Marriages (%)	Total (%)
	with 1st Gen.	with 2nd Gen.		
Males				
Native stock	68		32	100
Germans:				
1st Gen.	42	20	38	100
2nd Gen.	40	59	1	100
Danes:				
1st Gen.	83	13	4	100
2nd Gen.	0	40	60	100
Females				
Native stock	68		32	100
Germans:				
1st Gen.	49	36	15	100
2nd Gen.	21	52	27	100
Danes:				
1st Gen.	74	0	26	100
2nd Gen.	10	44	46	100

Note: Figures rounded to conform to marginal tables.

of these people to the individuals in question. Thus, both demographic and socioeconomic factors must be integrated into a single model that would help to explain why people married outside of their own groups.

Socioeconomic Factors and
The Group Characteristics Model

Although many similarities can be seen between the individual and group characteristics models of causation, there is also a highly significant difference between the theoretical bases of the two. The individual model, discussed in Chapter 3, dealt only with the effects of each person's own traits on his or her decision on out-marriage. The group model, however, hinges on the demographic traits of potential in-group and out-group spouses and on the relationships between the socioeconomic characteristics of the members of those groups and those of the individuals under study. In essence, the group characteristics model assumes that a person's decision to out-marry was a function of (1) both the absolute and relative availability of out-group spouses, and (2) their desirability, as measured by the degree of affinity between their socioeconomic traits and those of the individual in question. Support for this latter point comes from the large group of sociological studies, beginning with the work of Kingsley Davis in 1941, that have demonstrated marked similarity in the social characteristics of mates.[12]

In regard to its demographic aspects, the model suggests that a person's decision to out-marry correlated positively with the number of potential out-group spouses who lived in the same county and negatively with the number of such in-group mates in the same area. Three independent variables represent these factors. The first two are simply the tallies of the numbers of out-group and in-group spouses who were available while the third is the percentage of all potential spouses in the county who were in-group members. The out-group total should have related positively to out-marriage; the in-group total and the in-group percentage should have done so negatively.

The remaining components of the model are its socioeconomic

aspects. Under a norm stipulating homogamy according to social qualities, most marriages would have occurred within nationality groups (as indeed they did), because immigrants from the same country or origin tended to bear similar social traits. Out-group marriages should have occurred between unusual people, socially more akin to the members of other groups than to members of their own. Under the group model, a person's decision to marry outside his or her own group should, therefore, have related negatively to the degree of similarity between that individual's attributes and those of his or her potential in-group mates and positively to the degree of similarity between the characteristics of that person and those of his or her potential out-group spouses.

The socioeconomic variables in this model measure the relative similarities between people and the in-group and out-group mates available to them in their own county marriage markets. The characteristics, measurable at the statewide level and pertaining to differences between individuals and their possible endogamous mates are (1) generation, (2) age, (3) previous marital condition, and (4) community size. Those representing differences between individuals and their out-group partners include the traits just named and religious and linguistic backgrounds. The former set should have related to out-marriage negatively; the latter, positively.[13]

Happily, the group-characteristics model proves more useful to understanding the causes of marital assimilation than did the individual-based model of Chapter 3. It demonstrates that it is equally as effective as its forerunner in dealing with Eastern Europeans, slightly more helpful in regard to the native-stock, and remarkably more important in understanding the marital selections of Western immigrants. In the first group, the variables used can explain about one-fifth of the variance between in-group and out-group marriage. Similar variables can account for just under 11% of the variance for the native stock. For the Westerners, however, the Adjusted R^2 stands at a full 31.2%, representing a substantial contribution to the explanation of why some members of this group married outsiders.

The most important of the demographic and socioeconomic factors that influenced Western immigrants include (1) the percentage of the potential spouses in their own groups who lived in communities similar in size to their own, (2) the similarly located proportions

Table 4.7. Multiple Regression Coefficients for
Out-Group Marriage and the Components of the Group-
Characteristics Model for Wisconsin Residents in 1910

	Native Stock		Western Immigrants		Eastern European Immigrants	
	B	β	B	β	B	β
Independent Variables						
Demographic						
In-group size	-.877	-.291	-.567	-.221	-.434	-.308
	(1031)[a]		(.028)		(.027)	
Out-group absolute size[b]	-.001[c]	-.077[c]	...	...	...	...
Individual/in-group						
Generation	...	...	-.124	-.095	...	...
			(.018)			
Previous marriage	...	...	...	...	-.221	-.215
					(.021)	
Community size	-.178	-.119	-.459	-.374	-.354	-.340
	(.017)		(.017)		(.022)	
Individual/out-group						
Previous marriage	.104	.052	...	...	...	...
	(.019)					
Religion[b]	...	...	...	...	.001	.077
					(.000)	
Language	-.271[c]	-.057[c]	...	...	.010	.084
	(.048)				(.002)	
Community size	.222	.135	.442	.265	...	...
	(.018)		(.018)			
Multiple R	.330		.558		.448	
Multiple R²	.109		.312		.201	
Adjusted R²	.109		.312		.200	
Standard error	.471		.414		.390	
Constant	.743		.688		.675	
Weighted n	9932		7376		3584	
n	611		598		373	

[a] (Standard errors of B coefficients in parentheses.)
[b] Figure an absolute total rather than a percentage.
[c] Figure in disagreement with the model.
All figures are significant at the .001 level.

of possible out-group mates, and (3) the proportion of all possible mates represented by members of their own group. As the model suggested, the first and third of these correlated negatively with exogamy while the second's relationship was positive. Although these variables clearly carried the most influence, one other important one, the percentage of in-group members whose generation matched the individual's, also acted in the anticipated (negative) manner.

For the Eastern Europeans, on the other hand, the key demographic and socioeconomic indicators are their community-size relationships to potential in-group spouses and their nationality's percentage of the total number of available mates. Also important to these people are the proportion of their own groups who were alike in their experience regarding previous marriage. All three of these variables correlated negatively with the decision to out-marry, but two minor factors related positively to that decision. These involved similarities between the Eastern Europeans and the religious affiliations and languages of their possible outgroup mates. For each of these variables, however, the model correctly predicted the nature of the correlations to the dependent variable of out-group marriage.

At the statewide level, therefore, the group characteristics model does tell much about why some immigrants out-married while others did not. Westerners were more likely to find exogamous mates when they lived in counties where few from their own groups but many from other groups resided in communities similar in size to their own. A relatively greater number of possible outgroup spouses also encouraged them to out-marry. Similarly, the group factors based on community size and relative availability of in-group and out-group mates, along with the one involving previous marriages, affected the mate selections of the Eastern Europeans. Thus, for Wisconsin's immigrants, such group characteristics did influence the rates of marital assimilation.

A similar analysis for the residents of Milwaukee produces somewhat different results, as Table 4.8 demonstrates. The basic findings remain firm: The model is useful in understanding why immigrants out-married, but is less helpful in regard to the native stock, whose Adjusted R^2 is only .072. Among the newcomers in the urban environment, however, the combined factors had a more

Table 4.8. Multiple Regression Coefficients for
Out-Group Marriage and the Components of the
Group-Characteristics Model for Milwaukee Residents in 1910

	Native Stock		Western Immigrants		Eastern European Immigrants	
	B	β	B	β	B	β
Independent Variables						
Demographic						
Out-Group %	...	...	1.124	.413	5.045	.406
			(.040)[a]		(.317)	
Individual/in-group						
Generation	...	...	...	...	-.490	-.315
					(.034)	
Previous marriage	...	...	...	...	-.451	-.227
					(.042)	
Occupational status	...	...	...	...	-.025	-.192
Individual/out-group						
Mixed parents	-.424[b]	-.218[b]	...	...	...	...
	(.070)					
Occupational status	.422	.094	.570	.156	.512	.129
	(.154)		(.054)		(.094)	
Language	1.520	.087	...	...	.137	.076
	(.624)				(.043)	
Multiple R	.275		.443		.581	
Multiple R²	.076		.196		.338	
Adjusted R²	.072		.196		.335	
Standard error	.464		.416		.338	
Constant	.831		-111.602		-503.179	
Weighted n	791		3653		1538	
n	57		364		158	

[a] (Standard errors of B coefficients in parentheses.)
[b] Figure in disagreement with the model.
The Native Stock figures are significant at the .005 level. Those for the two immigrant groups are significant at the .001 level.

powerful influence on Eastern Europeans than on Westerners. Whereas the model explains over a third of the variance (.335) for the former grouping, it covers only about a fifth (.196) for the latter. Thus, in Milwaukee the model is quite helpful in understanding why Eastern Europeans outmarried and moderately so for Western immigrants.

Among the Eastern Europeans, the relative availability of out-group spouses and the generational affinity factor matching individuals and their in-groups were the strongest variables. In-group relationships involving previous marriage and occupational status were also important, as to a lesser extent were the out-group factors based on occupation and language. For the Western immigrants, only two variables proved important: relative availability and occupational status in regard to the out-group. Thus, in the urban environment, demographic, rather than socioeconomic factors, were prime considerations.

As was the case for the individual-based model of Chapter 3, it is possible to use the community of Racine to retest the group characteristics model. Better defined religious and occupational variables are available there, as is the additional measure of home ownership.[14] Tables 4.9 and 4.10 compare the effects of the two sets of variables in two years, 1910 and 1915.

Comparisons of the odd-numbered and even-numbered columns of the two tables yield similar results. In both 1910 and 1915, the introduction of new variables—those used in Columns 2, 4, and 6 —cause the Adjusted R^2s to rise in the cases of the native stock and the Eastern Europeans but to fall for the Western immigrants. For the native stock, the change is hardly significant, however, since the Adjusted R^2s remain low in both years. The figures for the other two groups are larger, and they change markedly. Their changes suggest that the use of the original variables in the state-wide and Milwaukee analyses may have caused distortions. In fact, the earlier findings may have resulted in overstatements of the model's usefulness for Westerners and understated its appropriateness for Eastern Europeans. For the former, the group characteristics model may actually explain somewhat less than the 31.2% (statewide) and 19.6% (Milwaukee) claimed. For the latter, it may account for more than the 20.0% and 33.5% (statewide and Milwaukee, respectively) credited to it.

In regard to the 1910 Western immigrants, the use of the new variables upsets the ranking order of only the less relevant

Table 4.9. Multiple Regression Coefficients for
Out-Group Marriage and the Components of the Group
Characteristics Model in Racine in 1910

	Native Stock		Western Immigrants		Eastern European Immigrants	
	1	2	3	4	5	6
	β	β	β	β	β	β
Independent variables						
Individual/in-group						
Generation	...	...	...	-.083 (.122)[a]	...	-.126 (.138)
Age	...	...	-.064 (.009)	...	...	...
Previous marriage	.032[b] (.344)	...	-.076 (.177)		...	-.086 (.241)
FC occupation	...	...	...	...	...	-.213 (.089)
PC home ownership	...	...	...	-.160 (.100)	...	...
Individual/out-group						
Generation	...	...	.566 (.283)	.378 (.305)	.556 (.553)	.381 (.526)
Age	-.148[b] (.020)	-.121[b] (.018)	...	...	.294 (.012)	.222 (.010)
Religion (Wisconsin def.)	...	...	.076 (.414)	...	-.137[b] (1.313)	...
Religion (Racine def.)	...	...	...	.077 (.331)	...	.102 (.200)
Language	...	...	.136 (.440)	.203 (.361)	.086 (.696)	...
FC occupation	...	-.060[b] (.209)	...	-.111[b] (.112)	...	...
PC home ownership	...	-.079 (.198)	...	...	...	...
Multiple R	.137	.174	.631	.530	.522	.585
Multiple R²	.019	.030	.398	.281	.272	.342
Adjusted R²	.008	.008	.382	.267	.249	.312
Standard error	.497	.497	.395	.428	.339	.347
Constant	.389	.612	-.931	-.594	-.455	-.095
n	90	90	150	252	97	117

[a] (Standard errors of B coefficients in parentheses.)
[b] Figure in disagreement with the model.

Table 4.10. Multiple Regression Coefficients for
Out-Group Marriage and the Components of the Group
Characteristics Model in Racine in 1915

	Native Stock		Western Immigrants		Eastern European Immigrants	
	1	2	3	4	5	6
	β	β	β	β	β	β
Independent Variables						
Individual/in-group						
Generation	...	...	...	...	...	-.208 (.54)[a]
Age	-.088 (.012)	-.084 (.012)	-.080 (.006)	-.146 (.005)	...	...
Previous marriage	.210[b] (.263)	.201[b] (.261)	...	.124[b] (.156)	-.094 (.160)	...
PC home ownership	...	.170[b] (.320)	...	...	...	-.108 (.120)
Individual/out-group						
Generation	...	...	.295 (.470)	.208 (.464)	.288 (.426)	.156 (.491)
Previous marriage	...	...	...	...	...	-.107[b] (.163)
Religion (Rac. def.)	...	...	...	...	...	.174 (.367)
Language	...	...	.268 (.605)	.099 (.470)	.187 (.484)	.182 (.513)
FC occupation	...	-.141[b] (.205)	...	-.055[b] (.149)	...	...
Multiple R	.194	.279	.417	.288	.343	.452
Multiple R²	.038	.078	.174	.083	.117	.205
Adjusted R²	.028	.050	.162	.067	.106	.180
Standard error	.493	.488	.460	.480	.386	.383
Constant	.042	-.061	-.664	-.514	-.453	.044
n	103	103	135	235	153	165

[a] (Standard errors of B coefficients in parentheses.)
[b] Figure in disagreement with the model.

variables in the group model. Though slightly reduced in importance, the out-group generational figure continues to have the greatest influence on the out-marriage decision. Language relationships between individuals and these out-groups, a factor whose beta coefficient rises when the new variables appear, retains its second position. The relative importance of the other variables, however, changes completely with the introduction of the new indicators. Under the statewide variables, the out-group factor of religion and the in-group ones for previous marriage and age were next. With the new variables in operation, in-group home ownership ranks third, followed by out-group occupational status, in-group generation, and the newly defined indicator for out-group religion. Among these, incidentally, only out-group occupational status failed to correlate with out-marriage in the manner suggested by the model.

Among the 1915 Westerners, out-group generational relationships were the most important, regardless of the type of variables used. With the new indicators in place, in-group factors based on age and previous marriage (the latter in disagreement with the model) moved past out-group language relationships as the next most relevant. For the Western immigrants of both years, therefore, the out-group generational factors were most influencial, but the relative importance of the others depended on the type of variables in use.

Table 4.9 shows that the same kind of situation prevails for the Eastern Europeans of 1910. Under both sets of variables, out-group generational and age factors were most important, but the relative value of the other factors changes completely when the new variables go into the analysis.

For the 1915 Eastern Europeans, however, switching indicators completely revises the rank order of the independent factors. With the statewide variables, the out-group factors for generation and language are most valuable to understanding out-marriage. Using the new variables creates a new ranking, headed by the in-group generational factor and followed by the out-group ones for language and religion. The choice of variables, therefore, does affect the relative importance of the factors that influenced the Eastern Europeans.

Unfortunately, it is impossible to determine the effects of using the original set of variables in the statewide and Milwaukee analyses. According to the Racine findings, it seems likely that the most important factors would have retained much of their influence, despite any changes induced by redefining some of the independent variables. It seems equally likely, however, that the original variable set may distort the value of some of the lesser factors. Conclusions must be drawn with this caution in mind.

The Composite Characteristics Model

Both personal and group traits did affect the would-be marriers among Wisconsin's immigrants, but the extent to which either set of factors influenced in-marriage and out-marriage depended on the nationality grouping in question. The individual characteristics approach adds to our understanding of out-marriage among Eastern European immigrants, while the group-based analysis provides useful information about both groups of newcomers. What remains then is to combine the approaches into a single composite model, explaining the extent to which demographic and socioeconomic factors affected marital assimilation. The result is an expansion of the overall explanatory power of some of the previous models, especially those concerning the Eastern Europeans, along with several changes in the relative importance of some of the particular variables.

Table 4.11 demonstrates the utility of the final composite model for explaining intermarriage at the statewide level. Although the composite model produces only a slight increase in the Adjusted R^2 for the native stock, it appears somewhat more useful in understanding the Western immigrants and distinctly more helpful in analyzing the Eastern Europeans. Again, given the many intangibles involved in mate selection, these figures, particularly those of the immigrant groups, represent notable contributions to understanding the causes of marital assimilation.

The relative influence of the independent variables that influenced the Western immigrants are much the same under both the group and composite models. Table 4.12 shows that the community-size variables involving both in-groups and out-groups are still the most important, followed by the in-group's relative size. In the composite model, however, mixed parentage becomes the fourth factor. Again, every independent factor considered related to out-group marriage in the predicted manner.

Table 4.11. Adjusted Multiple R^2s Resulting from Regression
Analyses of Out-Group Marriage, Using Individual, Group, and
Composite Models for Wisconsin Residents in 1910

National-/ Origin Groups	Individual Characteristics Model	Group Characteristics Model	Composite Characteristics Model
Native Stock	.005	.109	.110
Western immigrants	.100	.312	.328
Eastern European immigrants	.200	.200	.272

Among the Eastern Europeans, switching to the composite model results in a number of changes. For example, although the community-size variable relating to the in-groups and the relative sizes of those groups remain the chief influence on out-group marriage, the two variables reverse their positions relative to one another. In the composite model, the percentages of all potential mates represented by in-group members becomes the most important of the factors examined. After these come indicators of generation, previous marital condition, and membership in three social classes: lower-middle, upper-middle, and upper. Almost all of these factors correlate either negatively or positively to out-group marriage in the manner that the model predicted. The one exception is lower-middle social status.

Conversion to the composite model in Milwaukee causes just the opposite effects to those exhibited at the statewide level. In the urban environment, the analysis of the native stock gains the most by the composite approach. In the case of that group, the Adjusted R^2 grows from about 13% (individual model) to nearly 19%. The figure for the Westerners, however, remains unchanged, whereas that of the Eastern Europeans grows only about three percentage points to roughly 36%. Apparently, the group characteristics model was all one needed for understanding the demographic and social motives of Milwaukee's Western immigrants. Similarly, the group characteristics model is clearly the key to understanding the city's Eastern Europeans.

Table 4.12. Multiple Regression Coefficients for
Out-Group Marriage and the Components of the Composite
Model for Wisconsin Residents in 1910

	Native Stock		Western Immigrants		Eastern European Immigrants	
	B	β	B	β	B	β
Independent Variables						
Demographic						
In-group size	-.873	-.290	-.593	-.210	-.256	-.374
	(.032)[a]		(.028)		(.023)	
Individual						
Generation	...	...	...	...	.213	.230
					(.013)	
Parents' marriage	...	...	.138	.130	...	...
			(.010)			
Occupational class						
Upper	...	...	...	...	.619	.071
					(.126)	
Upper-middle	...	...	...	...	.333	.100
					(.047)	
Lower-middle	-.319	-.075	...	...	.730[b]	.118[b]
	(.041)				(.089)	
Individual/in-group						
Generation	...	...	-.106	-.081	...	...
			(.018)			
Previous marriage	...	...	...	...	-.208	-.202
					(.020)	
Community size	-.186	-.125	-.458	-.374	-.315	-.302
	(.017)		(.017)		(.021)	
Individual/out-group						
Previous marriage	.114	.056	...	...	...	...
	(.019)					
Religion[c]	-.001[b]	.080[b]	...	...	...	...
	(.000)					
Community size	.212	.129	.449	.269	...	...
	(.018)		(.018)			
Multiple R	.333		.573		.523	
Multiple R²	.111		.328		.273	
Adjusted R²	.110		.328		.272	
Standard error	.471		.409		.372	
Constant	.730		.618		.390	
Weighted n	9932		7376		3584	
n	611		598		373	

[a] (Standard errors of B coefficients in parentheses.)
[b] Figure in disagreement with the model.
[c] Figure an absolute total rather than a percentage.
All figures significant at the .001 level.

Table 4.13. Adjusted Multiple Rs Resulting from Regression
Analyses of Out-Group Marriage Using Individual, Group,
and Composite Models for Milwaukee Residents in 1910

National-Origin Groups	Individual Characteristics Model	Group Characteristics Model	Composite Characteristics Model
Native Stock	.128	.072	.186
Western immigrants	.092	.196	.196
Eastern European immigrants	.214	.335	.363

As Table 4.14 demonstrates, the model is not quite so helpful
for understanding native-stock Americans as the rather impressive
Adjusted R^2 seems to indicate. The problem lies in the nature of
the relationships between out-marriage and (1) upper-middle class
status, and (2) the out-group factor for parents' marriage. According to the model, both should have correlated positively with out-
marriage, but in fact the opposite was true. Moreover, as noted
earlier, it is difficult to put much faith in results based on so small
a sample size; in Milwaukee, as at the broader level, these models
explain more about immigrants than about the native stock.

For the Western immigrants, the equations for the group and
composite models are identical. Adding individual factors has vir-
tually no effect on the Adjusted R^2.

Combining the two original models does, however, cause some
changes in the rank order of the particular variables affecting the
Eastern Europeans. For them, the relative availability of out-group
spouses was most important, followed by the in-group generational
factor, the matter of previous marriage, and the factor involving
the occupational status of potential out-group spouses. Each of
these, along with the other significant factors noted, related to
out-marriage in the predicted manner. Thus, for both groups of
Milwaukeeans, relative availability was the most influential demographic or social factor favorable to marital assimilation.

If Fanny Morawetz and Joseph Mrkvick, the young couple who
lived next door to one another, were typical of Wisconsin's out-
marrying immigrants, demographic and socioeconomic group

Table 4.14. Multiple Regression Coefficients for
Out-Group Marriage and the Components of the
Composite Model for Milwaukee Residents in 1910

	Native Stock		Western Immigrants		Eastern European Immigrants	
	B	β	B	β	B	β
Independent Variables						
Demographic						
Out-group %	2.279	.107	1.124	.413	4.749	.382
	(1.001)[a]		(.040)		(.290)	
Individual						
Previous marriage	...	...	...	...	.438	.228
					(.040)	
Occupational class						
Upper	.246	.114	...	...	...	...
	(.073)					
Upper-middle	-.390[b]	-.327[b]	...	...	.264	.142
	(.045)				(.041)	
Middle	...	...	...	...	-.123	-.133
					(.022)	
Individual/in-group						
Generation	...	...	...	...	-.529	-.340
					(.033)	
Occupational class	-.076	-.231	...	...	-.018	-.134
	(.016)				(.003)	
Individual/out-group						
Parents' marriage	-.422[b]	-.217[b]	...	...	...	...
	(.065)					
Occupational class	...	...	.570	.156	.875	.220
			(.054)		(.098)	
Multiple R	.438		.443		.605	
Multiple R²	.192		.196		.366	
Adjusted R²	.186		.196		.363	
Standard error	.434		.416		.331	
Constant	-226.471		-111.603		-474.475	
Weighted n	791		3653		1538	
n	57		364		158	

[a] (Standard errors of B coefficients in parentheses.)
[b] Figure in disagreement with the model.
The Native Stock figures are significant at the .005 level. Those for the two immigrant groups are significant at the .001 level.

factors could explain in part their decision to marry across nationality lines. Similarly, if Jenny Thorgersen and Victor Christensen could represent the many in-marrying newcomers, then these same factors should help explain their decision. To be sure, personal factors—those based on personalities as well as those centered on the social traits of individuals—played an important role. So, too, did proximity. But such influences do not tell the whole story. Group factors also played a role by defining the number and the desirability of potential in-group and out-group mates.

As a member of the German Group, Franny Morawetz was a Western immigrant, as were the Danish Jenny Thorgersen and Victor Christensen. Each of these three may have felt more at ease with someone from a small city background like their own. Each consciously or subconsciously may have sought a mate from among small city people—a group which, in Racine County, may have included relatively few Germans but a larger number of Danes and members of other nationalities. Based on the statewide findings, it seems likely that such factors might have encouraged Franny to out-marry with someone like Joseph Mrkvicka while at the same time edging Jenny and Victor toward an endogamous match. Moreover, in terms of simple numbers, Franny probably had fewer in-group choices than either Jenny or Victor and this too may have been important.

If these individuals were typical Wisconsinites, this would be probable, though admittedly the specific analyses of the Racine data suggest that other factors may have entered into their decision-making.

Similarly, as an Eastern European immigrant, Czech-American Joseph Mrkvicka, according to the statewide findings, probably was influenced by a lack of Bohemian females from communities of Racine's size or, for that matter, from Racine. Again, though, other factors—those listed in Tables 4.9 and 4.10 for Eastern Europeans—may have been more important.

Regardless of the specifics, the central point is clear. Mate selection must be seen in a social context. Both the availability and desirability of prospective mates did substantially affect whether an individual married inside or outside his or her own group.

CHAPTER 5

The Melting Pot
and the Altar: Conclusions

By most standards, Robert M. La Follette and Belle Case were extraordinary people, yet in selecting each other as marriage partners, they acted in a predictable manner. The future governor and United States senator and the soon-to-be first female graduate of the University of Wisconsin Law School discovered one another on the Madison campus, in an era when higher education remained largely the province of native-stock Americans such as themselves. Given the geographic limits on his courtship activities, the non-immigrant environment of the university, and his own social characteristics and their relationship to those of the women around him, Bob La Follette's choice of a native-stock American like Belle Case hardly came as a surprise. Nor was it unusual for women with traits like hers to seek out a native-stock man. Their endogamous marriage, in fact, illustrates many of the ways in which demographic and socioeconomic factors combined to sway the judgments of marriageable individuals toward either in-group or out-group unions.

Born 24 miles southwest of Madison in a double log cabin built by his father in the town of Primrose, Bob La Follette was a "local boy who made good." He grew up on the family farm under the

115

guidance of his mother and stern stepfather. At the age of 18 in 1873, Bob moved his thrice-widowed mother and sister Josephine to a small farm on the outskirts of the capital city so that he could take a year of preparatory work and qualify for admission to the university. It was during his second year (1874-1875) in Madison that he met the 16-year-old freshman Belle Case.[1]

By the time that he and Belle became secretly engaged at the end of their junior year in college, Bob La Follette had won a considerable reputation as an orator, editor, and political activist. Since his arrival on campus, Bob had joined the Athenae literary and debating society (such clubs then serving as major centers for social activities), purchased and run the student newspaper, the *University Press,* and thrown himself into a struggle against secret fraternities. Like other undergraduates, however, he was not so well-known off-campus, and his range of social acquaintances, in all likelihood, did not extend much past the boundaries of his home county.[2]

Belle Case's origins differed little from those of her future husband. Like him, she had been born in a log cabin in rural Wisconsin, a child of native-born parents. When she was only three years of age, her family moved from her birthplace in Juneau County to the village of Baraboo in Sauk County. On graduating from high school there, the highly independent young Belle entered the university in the fall of 1874.[3] A talented student of history and Latin, she too became interested in rhetoric and joined a literary society that rivaled Bob's own club. In 1878, she thoroughly impressed her suitor with an oration that she delivered at the state capitol on the subject of "Children's Playthings."[4] Bob raved about the performance in the pages of the *University Press.* It was clear to him that he had found in Belle the woman that he wanted for his wife. Although hesitant at first, Belle finally agreed to the match, and in the spring of 1879, they publicly announced their plans for marriage.[5]

Hard pressed for money, the young couple soon decided to postpone their nuptials. After graduation, Belle returned to her hometown and taught school for two years while her fiancé began studying law in the Madison office of R. M. Bashford (later a justice of the Wisconsin Supreme Court). Only seven months after

commencement, Bob passed the state bar exam and in the following year he ran for and won the office of District Attorney for
Dane County. With his election victory came the salary that the
young couple needed to set up their household. Bob now earned
what seemed to his small-town bride a princely sum: $800 annual-
ly, not to mention a $50 allowance for expenses.[6]

Still the pair hardly rushed to the altar. Over a year passed
between the election and their wedding day. Perhaps that period
provided time for reflection, especially for the bride-to-be, since
Bob, it appears, had already married his career. For example, even
though he and Belle had decided to wed on New Year's Eve of
1881, he insisted in remaining in Madison until late afternoon in
order to prosecute a case in court. Fortunately, he took the time
to jot himself a note ("Five p.m. Go to Baraboo") so he remem-
bered to leave in sufficient time to arrive at the Case home on
schedule. Immediately after a Unitarian minister pronounced them
"husband and wife" in a ceremony that, incidentally, excluded the
word "obey" from the bride's vows, the Robert La Follettes
caught a train back to Madison, presumably so that the new groom
would miss as little time as possible from his work.[7]

When Bob La Follette and Belle Case became engaged, they did
exactly as most young people of their nationality in selecting in-
group mates. In the 12-month period immediately following their
graduation from the university, roughly 70% of all native-stock
Americans who married in Wisconsin chose their marriage partners
from their own nationality group. That fact alone carries the im-
plication that endogamous marriage was the accepted practice
among people like these two.

In-group marriages appeared even more often among the mem·
bers of the Western nationalities of that period. For example, over
88% of the Wisconsin marriers who came to America from Norway and fully 85% of the United States-born brides and grooms
with Norwegian parents selected their mates from that same nationality.[8] Thus, the odds were substantial that an enterprising,
young, second-generation Norwegian like Hank Hawkinson of the
Town of Dunn would select an in-group mate. It hardly came as a
surprise when he married Carrie Larson, a resident of Pleasant
Springs, but a native of Norway.[9] Similarly, among the Germans,

who together with the Norwegians comprised over half of all of the 1880 immigrants in the state, about 86% and 80% of the first and second generations, respectively, married other Germans.

In-group marriage was also the usual occurrence among the Irish and, although just barely so, among natives of Great Britain. Neither of these groups, however, proved nearly as endogamous as the Norwegians and Germans. Robert Keenan, a second-generation Irishman from the Village of Oregon, and English-born Sara Carrison of Rutland probably caused only minor comment when they contracted marriage with native-stock Americans, Ella York and O. F. Flint.[10] After all, only 63% of the second-generation British married endogamously.

Only among the second-generation British and the Canadians did majorities select marriage partners from outside groups. Yet, even in these cases, about 40% still married endogamously. Thus, with only minor exceptions, majorities of nearly all of the nationalities in 1880 behaved as Bob La Follette and Belle Case in choosing their mates from among the members of their own national-origin groups.

The endogamous percentages of these same groups, however, dropped considerably by 1910. In that year, shoemaker Ben Rice's choice of another native-stock American, a servant named Abbie Thompson, was no more typical of the selections of others of their nationality than was Hattie Hostler's choice of William Mueller, a Madison factory worker from the German state of Westphalia.[11] Only a bare majority of 51% of the Americans of native parentage who married in that year settled down with such native-stock mates.

Among the Western immigrants of 1910, only the Norwegians and Germans had more people who married within their own groups than outside of them. About 70% of the Norwegian first-generation and roughly 54% of the second married endogamously, while the corresponding German totals were 76% and 55%, respectively. Both of these sets of figures, however, fell below their groups' 1880 marks. Of the smaller Western nationalities present in both years, the highest in-group percentages for each generation were the rather low figures (39% and 22%, respectively) of the British second and Canadian first generations. Small majorities of the first-generation Swedes and Danes found in-group marriage partners, but only 32% and 23% of their respective second generations did so. Thus, the 1910 marriage of German-born machinist William Laplich was normal in that his bride, a 21-year-old factory worker named Frieda Vogal, also came from German stock.[12] Among the Irish, however, Dan Lynch's union with Mary Zwittler was equally typical. This Irish-American farmer from Vermont, Wisconsin, looked beyond his own group in choosing the second-generation Austrian.[13]

The in-group marriage of Jane Schnid and dentist B. Hailin, on the other hand, could well represent those of nearly 80% or more of the first-generation members of the Eastern European group. Although both the future bride and her 22-year-old fiancé made their homes in Madison, each had come to this country from their native Russia.[14]

Relatively high endogamy also persisted among the second-generation Poles and Russians, their in-group proportions running 81% and 67%, respectively. The native-born children of Bohemian and Austrian newcomers, such as Mary Zwittler, however, proved much more likely to find out-group mates. In each of these cases, only about 30% married endogamously.

In regard to the proportions who married within and outside of their own groups, therefore, apparent differences can be seen among the Western and Eastern European immigrant groupings. The fairly high 1880 endogamy rates of the Westerners, as well as that of the native stock, all declined by 1910, with some even falling below 50%. The Eastern European rates, however, were significantly higher than these latter figures, though roughly parallel to those of the Norwegians and Germans of the earlier year. Thus, while the differences were real, they seem due at least in part to the much earlier arrival in Wisconsin of the Western immigrants. Moreover, the location of a larger percentage of the former newcomers in the more rural areas of the state, where marital assimilation was more likely, further helps to explain the differences in the out-marriage rates of the two groups. With time and place considered, the differences were not overly important.

To what extent, then, can we explain "why?" Why did many individuals do as Dan Lynch and Mary Zwittler and marry across nationality lines while others, such as Jane Schnid and B. Hailin, married endogamously? Chapters 3 and 4 offered some of the answers as they analyzed demographic and individual social factors.

Chapter 3, in particular, examined the traits of individuals to see whether people with certain characteristics were more likely than others to out-marry. Unfortunately, as Tables 3.1 and 3.2 demonstrated, the individual characteristics measurable at the statewide level revealed little about why Western immigrants like William Mueller and William Laplich out-married and in-married, respectively. In fact, these personal traits seem to have had little impact on both native-stock and Western immigrants, a finding that holds true for the state as a whole and for Milwaukee. Even if more specifically defined characteristics were available statewide, as they were in Racine, they likely would not have altered the findings for these two groups (see Tables 3.3 and 3.4), for the other factors weighed much heavier in the intermarriage decision.

In the case of Eastern Europeans such as Mary Zwittler and Jane Schnid, however, the personal attributes of the marriers proved somewhat more important. Both statewide and in Milwaukee, these characteristics were capable of explaining about 20% of the variance in the out-marriage decision. Moreover, this finding may itself have understated the relevance of such factors. Based on the Racine analysis, better defined characteristics alone might have caused that 20% figure to rise to some more significant mark.

At the statewide level, the most important factors promoting intermarriage were those that increased the likelihood that the individual had been exposed to cultures other than his own. In this regard, Mary Zwittler is a good example, because of her second-generation status. As the native-born child of Austrian parents Florian and Agnes Zwittler, she probably grew up in the Badger State. Her chances of learning about other cultures, and of meeting men from other groups, such as Dan Lynch, must surely have been greater than those of people like Jane Schnid who were born abroad. This may well have been one reason why Mary chose a mate from another national group and her Russian counterpart did not. In the same respect, Mary Zwittler's chances of out-marriage probably would have been even greater had her parents come from different countries. This factor, another indication of cultural diversity, also ranked high in importance, followed by middle-class occupational status.

Had these Eastern European immigrants lived in Milwaukee, an upper-middle class occupation probably would have proved most influential in encouraging them to out-marry. It would have been followed in turn by second-generation status and, rather unexpectedly, by the lower-middle occupational level. The lower-middle ranking, which correlated positively in both the statewide and Milwaukee analyses, represents the one factor whose effect was the opposite of that theorized. Otherwise, the results of Tables 3.2 and 3.3 confirm suspicions about the effects of individual characteristics on the decision to out-marry.

Chapter 4 did not concentrate on the marriers themselves, but rather on the relationships between them and their prospective in-group and out-group spouses. Attention focused on "marriage markets," defined as the counties in which the individual marriers lived. Since at least three-quarters of the marriers of each major grouping found their mates within their own counties, this seemed a reasonable definition for the areas within which would-be marriers sought their mates.[15]

Within these markets, the availability and desirability of potential mates proved to be strong influences on mate selection. In regard to the former, Chapter 4 examined the role of demographic factors based on group sizes and sex ratios in limiting the numbers of possible in-group and out-group mates. The statistical tool of iterative rescaling demonstrated the importance of these elements in the largest groups in the Milwaukee and Racine marriage markets (see Tables 4.3-4.6), thereby suggesting that the same demographic factors probably functioned elsewhere in the state.

The individuals mentioned earlier demonstrate the central point. For example, the relative abundance of potential in-group mates may well have encouraged native-stock Americans, such as Ben Rice and Abbie Thompson to in-marry. A similar availability may have affected the choices of Germans, such as William Laplich and Frieda Vogal and, perhaps, even Russians such as Jane Schnid and B. Hailin. At the same time, however, Dane County may have offered considerably fewer in-group possibilities for Irishman Dan Lynch and Austrian Mary Zwittler. If this were the case, these demographic realities may well have contributed to their cross-nationality marriages.

Chapter 4 also considered the extent to which social desirability, based on measures of social affinity, affected marital assimilation. This analysis tested the proposition that in-group marriage depended in part on social homogamy. That is, that similarity between an individual and his or her potential in-group spouses encouraged in-group marriage while dissimilarities promoted out-marriages. Conversely, exogamy was most likely to occur under the unusual conditions where an individual was socially akin to potential out-group mates but unlike those from his or her in-group.

As Tables 4.7 and 4.8 demonstrated, this reasoning, fortified by the concept of demographic pressures, proved sound in the cases of two of the three groups, the Western and Eastern European immigrants. At the statewide level, the resulting multiple regression equations proved capable of explaining over 30% and over 20% of the variances for the two groups, respectively. In Milwaukee, the figures were roughly reversed—about 20% in the case of the Westerners and over 33% for the Eastern Europeans. As Tables 4.9 and 4.10 showed, however, the Racine data raise the possibility that the particular variables used may overstate the importance of group relationships in the case of the Westerners, while at the same time understating them for the Eastern Europeans.

For people such as Dan Lynch and William Mueller—Westerners who out-married—the key factors were the numbers of potential in-group and out-group spouses who lived in communities similar in size to their own. For Lynch, there were probably few Irish but a number of non-Irish women who lived in the rural areas of Dane County. This availability may have hastened his choice of an Austrian farm girl, Mary Zwittler. Mueller may have discovered few German females in Madison, but a good number of marriagable females from other nationality groups—an encouragement to him to choose one of them, Hattie Hostler, as his bride. Similarly, there may have been rather few Irish and German maids in the whole county, regardless of the sizes of their communities. As Table 4.7 demonstrated, availability also may have had a bearing on the decisions of Lynch and Mueller. If they had been Milwau-keeans, however, as Table 4.8 showed, the single most important group influence would have been the relative number of out-group members among all possible spouses.

The community size variable as it related to the in-group (though surprisingly not to the out-groups) also played an impor-tant role in the decisions of the Eastern Europeans. This factor, along with the absolute number of possible in-group mates, had the strongest effects on people such as Jane Schnid and Mary Zwittler. The presence of a number of Russian men in Madison and Dane Counties may have encouraged the former to pick a Russian mate. A corresponding inaccessibility of Austrian men may have been influential in the latter's out-marriage. Again, if these two had lived in Milwaukee, it is likely that the most impor-tant of these factors for them probably would have been the per-centage of out-group spouses available, followed by the in-group generational variable.

Chapter 4 combined the earlier findings about individual and group characteristics into one composite explanation of the socio-economic factors that affected intermarriage. This final approach demonstrated the rather strong influence that these factors had on the decision-making of Wisconsin's Western and Eastern European immigrants, both in the state as a whole and in Milwaukee in parti-cular. Statewide, these factors had a stronger effect on the West-erners, explaining roughly a third of the variance as opposed to just over a quarter in the case of the Eastern Europeans. In Mil-waukee, the situation was the reverse. There the same character-istics provided a better explanation for out-marriages among the Eastern Europeans (Adjusted R^2 = .363) than among the Western immigrants (Adjusted R^2 = .196).

As noted earlier, community size in relation to both in-groups and out-groups, the relative availability of in-group spouses, and mixed parents were the specific characteristics most influential to the state's Western newcomers such as Lynch and Mueller. Other factors were more important to Eastern Europeans such as Zwittler and Hailin. These included the relative number of potential in-group mates; the community-size factor in regard to the same group; and the individual traits of generation, previous marital status, and lower-middle, upper-middle, and upper-class statuses. In Milwaukee, no important changes were noted in the influences on the Westerners, but among Eastern Europeans, a slightly revised list included the absolute number of available out-group spouses, generational status in relation to the in-group, previous marital status, and occupational similarity to the out-group.

When surveyed from the vantage point of the marriage altar, therefore, the old concept of an American "melting pot" regains its respectability. Large percentages of immigrants, at least in early twentieth-century Wisconsin, did indeed find mates beyond the boundaries of their own nationality groups. This behavior was more true of Western immigrants than of those from Eastern Europe, not because of any innate ability to adjust to new environments, but rather, in a large measure, was owing to their earlier arrivals, relatively larger second-generation components, and less urban locations.

Such findings suggest that recent studies stressing cultural and structural pluralism—certainly important tendencies in the development of many groups—may have improperly deemphasized the assimilative side of immigrant life in America. Since many recent works have focused on the first-generation experiences of later arriving groups located in urban areas, it is hardly surprising that they say less about assimilation than about interethnic community life.[16] From this study, it seems likely that such works have focused on the very people least likely to intermix with native-stock Americans or with members of other immigrant groups. This emphasis is fine, of course, as long as such studies do not generate a broad notion that assimilation was rare. At least in Wisconsin, this was not the case.

As suggested by the theory developed in the introduction, people's decision to marry outside their own groups resulted from the pressures of several independent factors. For example, the earlier contention that greater exposure to alien cultures enhanced the likelihood of intermarriage held true for the Eastern Europeans. Although such contact was a minor factor for other groups, cultural awareness seems to have encouraged these people to look beyond their own groups for marriage partners. Such a finding suggests that Milton Gordon and his followers may have put aside the notion of acculturation too quickly. At least in this instance, acculturation seemed to have encouraged intermarriage and thus contributed to the overall process of assimilation.

The theory also suggested that the relative availability and social similarity of eligible out-group members should have encouraged intermarriage. This idea proved correct for both of the major immigrant groupings. Such a finding, however, does not counter Gordon's theory of the importance of structural assimilation. Indeed, when more out-group than in-group people were available, and when they were more similar to the person in question than members of his or her own group, structural assimilation probably occurred. Thus, it is likely that Gordon was correct in assuming that such mixing led to intermarriage. On this point, the present study supplements his work by suggesting conditions that encouraged such assimilation and amalgamation.

The remaining independent factor in the theory is the immeasurable one, group norms. Clearly, these norms influenced the immigrant people of Wisconsin and accounted to some extent for the remaining variance in the equations. If personal preferences balanced one another, that is, if such preferences resulted in like numbers of in-group and out-group matings, then group norms would have been the major unknown factor. In the statewide analysis normative pressures would have been stronger on the Eastern Europeans than on the Westerners, with the reverse holding true in the big city environment of Milwaukee. The norms would have had a great influence on both groups, however, for there was much to the out-marriage decision that the various independent factors failed to explain. Although this deduction seems logical, it can never be certain until researchers can measure personal preferences — not an imminent prospect.

The "melting pot" concept needs more attention, not less. The socioeconomic characteristics examined here tell only some of the reasons that people intermarried. Personal factors, especially psychological ones and ones involving parental control over marriage contracts, also deserve extended consideration. Although this study broadens the scope of assimilative inquiry from the local to the statewide level, the national story of intermarriage has yet to be told. This then represents but a beginning to a broad-scale understanding of the "melting pot" and the altar.

Notes and Selected Bibliography

Notes

Introduction: The Study of Marital Assimilation

1. Milwaukee County Marriage Records (manuscripts), Vol. 189 (1908), 194.

2. Richard Crowder, *Carl Sandburg* (New York, 1964), 39-41, and Gary F. Keller, "Carl Sandburg's Wisconsin Years," *Historical Messenger of the Milwaukee County Historical Society* 30 (Winter 1974), 106-116. The term "rabble-rouser" is from Keller, 108.

3. *Milwaukee Journal,* June 5, 1978, Part I, 8.

4. *Ibid.*

5. Crowder, 40.

6. See also Karl Detzer, *Carl Sandburg: A Study in Personality and Background* (New York, 1941) and Harry Golden, *Carl Sandburg* (Cleveland, 1961).

7. The phrase is from the title of Milton L. Barron's *The Blending American: Patterns of Intermarriage* (Chicago, 1972).

8. Julius Drachsler, *Democracy and Assimilation: The Blending of Heritages in America* (New York, 1920).

9. *Ibid.,* 87.

10. For example, see: Virginia Yans-McLaughlin, *Family and Community: Italian Immigrants in Buffalo, 1880-1930* (Ithaca, New York, 1977); Josef J. Barton, *Peasants and Strangers: Italians, Rumanians and Slovaks in an American City, 1890-1950* (Cambridge, Mass., 1975); Stephan Thernstrom, *The Other Bostonians: Poverty and Progress in the American Metropolis, 1880-1930: A Study in Ethnic Mobility* (New York, 1970); Howard P. Chudacoff, "A New Look at Ethnic Neighborhoods: Residential Dispersion and the Concept of Visibility in a Medium-Sized City," *Journal of American History* 60 (June 1973), 76-93; and Roger D. Simon, "Housing and Services in an Immigrant Neighborhood," *Journal of Urban History* 2 (August 1976), 435-458.

130   NOTES

11. Marriage registrations of the state of Wisconsin, 1850-1920 (manuscripts), State Office Building, Madison. These records appear on shelves, roughly by years (though earlier years are combined) and alphabetically by county. In the later years, including 1910, they also fall into town, village, and city categories within each county.

The data in Chapter 2 came from a one in three systematic sample of the 1890, 1900, and 1910 records and a one in two sample of those for 1920 when the number of foreign-born marriers tapered off. The totals for these samples are available on request from the author. The 1910 sample is much larger than those for previous years because its native-born component later subdivides into native-stock American and second-generation immigrants.

The 1910 sample used in Chapters 3 and 4 was also a stratified, systematic sample, but it was somewhat more complex than the others. This sample included: (1) one-third of the matches between native-born grooms and foreign-born brides; (2) one-ninth of the marriages involving a foreign-born groom and a native-born bride; (3) one-ninth of all marriages between two foreign-born people; and (4) one-eighteenth of all marriages between two native-born individuals. The resulting unweighted sample size included 2,966 individuals. Data from all samples used are available from the author.

Such marital data, taken from either marriage applications or marriage certificates (called "marriage records" here), is rare, indeed, and is almost never in central locations as is the Wisconsin data in Madison. In addition to the data noted here, similar information has appeared for the Province of Ontario, the city of Boston, and Santa Cruz County, California. See C. A. Price and J. Zubrzycki, "The Use of Intermarriage Statistics as an Index of Assimilation" *Population Studies* 16 (July 1962), 58-69.

12. In the calendar years of 1870 and 1880, the state of Wisconsin recorded 7,864 and 11,451 marriages, respectively, according to the United States Department of Labor, *A Report on Marriage and Divorce in the United States, 1867-1886* (Washington, February, 1889), Table I, 434-439. The manuscripts of the United States Census, however, contained only 2,371 and 2,736 marriages for 1869-70 and 1879-80, respectively. While the census takers clearly undercounted these unions, it is impossible to determine a bias in their figures against nuptials involving members of certain groups.

Chapter 2 uses all of these marriages without sampling. Elsewhere there are references to statewide data for 1880. These originate in a stratified, systematic sample from that year's census manuscripts. This sample included all marriages that involved a native-born groom and a foreign-born bride, and one-half of the remaining unions. Beginning with the first marriage listed, every other couple fell into the sample. The result of this procedure was a sample size of 3,514 people.

13. The best discussion of the melting pot concept and its relationship to Anglo-conformity and pluralism is in Milton Gordon, *Assimilation in American Life: The Role of Race, Religion and National Origins* (New York, 1964), 84-159.

14. J. Hector St. Jean de Crèvecoeur, *Letters from an American Farmer* (New York, 1925 edition), 54-55.

15. For a modernized version of this notion see Michael Novak, *The Rise of the Unmeltable Ethnics: Politics and Culture in the Seventies* (New York, 1971).

16. Gordon, *Assimilation,* 60-83.

17. Stanley Lieberson, *Ethnic Patterns in American Cities* (Glencoe, Ill., 1963); Steven M. Cohen, "Patterns of Ethnic Marriage and Friendship in the United States," Ph.D. thesis, Columbia University, 1974; and R. D. Alba, "Assimilation Among American Catholics," Ph.D. thesis, Columbia University, 1974. See also Cohen, "Socioecono-

mic Determinents of Interethnic Marriage and Friendship," *Social Forces,* cited here-after as *SF,* 55 (June 1977), 997-1010.

18. Edward Murguia and W. Parker Frisbie, "Trends in Mexican American Inter-marriage: Recent Findings in Perspective," *Social Science Quarterly* 58 (December 1977), 374.

19. Marcson, "A Theory of Intermarriage and Assimilation," *SF* 29 (October 1950), 75-78. Marcson, however, is not the only researcher to question this link. J. Milton Yinger and George Eaton Simpson, "The Integration of Americans of Indian Descent," *Annals of the American Academy of Political and Social Science* 436 (March 1978), 137-151, argue that intermarriage can be unrelated to other forms of assimilation. This situation occurs, however, only when one group has overwhelming power over another and forces individuals of the weaker group to behave in certain ways. While this theory may explain much about Indian-Anglo relations, it does not seem to apply to immigrant-native interactions.

20. *Ibid.,* 77-78.

21. For example, see W. D. Borrie, *The Cultural Integration of Immigrants* (Paris, 1959), 93-94.

22. Price and Zubrzycki, "Use."

23. Merton, "Intermarriage and the Social Structure: Fact and Theory," *Psychiatry* 4 (August 1941), 361-374.

24. Gordon, *Assimilation,* 60-83.

25. For examples, see Bessie Bloom Wessel, *An Ethnic Survey of Woonsocket, Rhode Island* (Chicago, 1931); Constantine Panunzio, "Intermarriage in Los Angeles, 1924-33," *American Journal of Sociology,* cited hereafter as *AJS,* 47 (March 1942), 690-701; Milton L. Barron, *People Who Intermarry, Intermarriage in a New England Industrial Community* (Syracuse, N.Y., 1946); August B. Hollingshead, "Cultural Fac-tors in the Selection of Marriage Mates," *American Sociological Review,* cited hereafter as *ASR,* 15 (October 1950), 619-627; John H. Burma, "Interethnic Marriage in Los Angeles, 1948-1959," *SF* 42 (December 1963), 156-165; Joseph P. Fitzpatrick, "Inter-marriage of Puerto Ricans in New York City," *AJS* 71 (January 1966), 395-406; Frank G. Mittelback and Joan W. Moore, "Ethnic Endogamy, The Case of Mexican Americans," *AJS* 74 (July 1968), 50-62; and Ulf Beijobom, *Swedes in Chicago: A Demographic and Social Study of the 1846-1880 Immigration* (Upsala, Sweden, 1971). The standard bibliography for intermarriage literature is Joan Aldous and Reuben Hill, *International Bibliography of Research in Marriage and the Family, 1900-1964,* with supplements (Minneapolis, 1967).

26. Douglas T. Gorak and Mary M. Kritz, "Intermarriage Patterns in the U.S.: Maximizing Information from the U.S. Census Public Use Samples," *Review of Public Data Use* 6 (March 1978), 33-43, suggest the use of national samples of married couples as an answer to this problem. Unfortunately, these samples comprise a "survivors index," with all the drawbacks discussed. For another approach based on selection of repre-sentative communities, see Sam Bass Warner, Jr. and Sylvia Fleisch, *Measurements for Social History: Metropolitan American, 1860-1960* (Beverly Hills, Calif., 1977).

27. Ruby Jo Reeves Kennedy: "Marriages in New Haven Since 1870, Statistically Analyzed and Culturally Interpreted," unpublished Ph.D. thesis, Yale University, 1938; "Single or Triple Melting-Pot? Intermarriage Trends in New Haven, 1870-1940," *AJS* 49 (January 1944), 331-339; "Single or Triple Melting Pot? Intermarriages in New Haven, 1870-1950," *AJS* 58 (July 1952), 56-59.

28. John L. Thomas, "The Factor of Religion in the Selection of Marriage Mates," *ASR* 16 (August 1951), 487-491.

29. No clear proof exists in the Wisconsin data of a Catholic melting pot at work. In 1910, for example, while about three-fourths of the out-marrying immigrants from Protestant countries married people with similar Protestant heritages, only 41.9% of the out-marrying grooms from Catholic origins and 26.7% of brides from the same countries selected mates from Catholic lands.

30. Hyman Rodman, "Technical Note on Two Rates of Mixed Marriage," *ASR* 30 (October 1965), 777.

31. Rodman provided a formula by which one can transform rates for marriages to rates for individuals and vice versa. Following Rodman's suggestion, all rates reported here are for individuals, not marriages.

32. Price and Zubrzycki, "Use."

33. Edmund de S. Brunner, *Immigrant Farmers and Their Children, With Four Studies of Immigrant Communities* (Garden City, N.Y., 1929), 75-91. Brunner's information came from marriage applications, which apparently continued in use in some rural counties after World War I. Most urban counties had by that time replaced them with forms having a more restricted format. The applications, as opposed to the marriage registrations, or records, used here, are not centrally located, and their continued existence depends on hundreds of county officials across the state.

34. This study follows others in utilizing those who did marry as surrogates for those eligible for marriage. Although not an entirely satisfactory method, this procedure makes possible the calculation of statewide marriage rates.

35. Glick, "Intermarriage and Fertility," and Paul H. Besanceney, "On Reporting Rates of Intermarriage," *AJS* 70 (May 1965), 717-721.

36. For example, see Hildegard Binder Johnson, "Intermarriages Between German Pioneers and Other Nationalities in Minnesota in 1860 and 1870," *AJS* 51 (January 1946), 229-304.

37. Stanley Lieberson, "The Price-Zubrzycki Measure of Ethnic Intermarriage," *Eugenics Quarterly* 13 (March 1966), 92-100.

38. Niles Carpenter, *Immigrants and their Children, 1920: A Study Based on Census Statistics Relative to the Foreign-Born and the Native White of Foreign or Mixed Parentage, Census Monographs, VII* (Washington, 1927).

39. The term "first-generation immigrant" denotes persons born outside the United States. "Second-generation immigrants," despite the connotation of the label, are the American-born children of first-generation immigrants. "Native-stock Americans" or "second-generation natives" are the native-born children of native-born parents.

40. Nelson, "Intermarriage," 591.

41. de Crévecoeur, *Letters from an American Farmer,* 55.

Chapter 1: Wisconsin's Immigrants

1. The statewide and county-level polulation totals appearing in Tables 1.1-1.3 and in the rest of the chapter originated in the following sources: Joseph Schafer, *Wisconsin Domesday Book, General Studies,* hereafter cited as *WDB,GS,* Vol. I: *A History of Agriculture in Wisconsin* (Madison, 1922), Figure 13 (page unnumbered), for selected 1850 county data on country of origin; the U.S. Censuses for 1850, Part II (Washington, 1853), Table XV, xxxvi-xxxvii; 1860, *Population* (Washington, 1864), 616-623; 1870,

Compendium (Washington, 1872), Table XVIII, 442; 1880, Vol. I: *Population* (Washington, 1883), Table XXVII, 691; 1890, *Compendium* (Washington, 1897), Table 3, 680-682 and Vol. I: *Population,* Part I (Washington, 1895), Table 38, 686-687; 1900, Vol. I: *Population,* Part I (Washington, 1902), Table 34, 793-795 and Table 40, 814-815; 1910, *Statistics for Wisconsin* (Washington, 1913), Table I, 602-615; 1920, Vol. II: *Population* (Washington, 1922), Table 8, 915; and the Wisconsin State Censuses for 1895, *Tabular Statements of the Census Enumeration and the Agricultural, Dairying and Manufacturing Interests of the State of Wisconsin, June 20, 1895,* Part I (Madison, 1895), 110-111; and 1905, *Ibid, June 1, 1905,* Part I (Madison, 1906), 264-265. Countries of birth and origin are available for Wisconsin urban populations in the U.S. Censuses for 1870, Vol. I: *Population* (Washington, 1872), Table VIII, 380-391; 1880, Vol. I, Table XVI, 538-541; 1890, Vol. I, Table 33, 610-669 and Table 34, 670-675; 1900, Vol. I, Table 35, 796-803; 1910, Vol. III: *Population* (Washington, 1913), Table II, 1096-1097; and 1920, Vol. II, Table 12, 729-731 and Table 17, 760-767.

2.   See note 39 of introduction.

3.   The estimate is based on a tally of Eastern European immigrant first- and second-generation totals as given and estimates of 60,000 and 18,000 second-generation Poles and Bohemians, respectively.

4.   Schafer, *WDB,GS,* Vols. I; II: *Four Wisconsin Counties: Prairie and Forest* (Madison, 1927); III: *The Wisconsin Lead Region* (Madison, 1932); and IV: *The Winnebago-Horicon Basin, A Type Study in Western History* (Madison, 1937); Alice E. Smith, *The History of Wisconsin, Vol. I: From Exploration to Statehood* (Madison, 1973), 464-498; Richard N. Current, *The History of Wisconsin, Vol. II: The Civil War Era, 1848-1873* (Madison, 1976), 42-82 and 117-145; Kathleen Neils Conzen, *Immigrant Milwaukee, 1836-1860: Accommodation and Community in a Frontier City* (Cambridge, Mass., 1976); William F. Whyte, "The British Element in Wisconsin," in Milo M. Quaife, *Wisconsin: Its History and its People, 1634-1924,* Vol. II (Chicago, 1924), 207-243; Louis A. Copeland, "The Cornish in Southwest Wisconsin," *Collections of the State Historical Society of Wisconsin,* hereafter cited as *Cols.,* 14 (Madison, 1898), 301-334; James A. Bryden, "The Scots in Wisconsin," *Proceedings of the State Historical Society of Wisconsin,* hereafter cited as *Pro.,* 1901 (Madison, 1901), 153-158; Anna Adams Dickie, "Scotch-Irish Presbyterian Settlers in Southern Wisconsin," *Wisconsin Magazine of History,* hereafter cited as *WMH,* 31 (March 1948), 291-304; Daniel J. Williams, *The Welsh Community of Waukesha County* (Columbus, Ohio, 1926); and Sadie Rowlands Price, "The Welsh of Waukesha County," *WMH* 26 (March 1943), 323-332.

5.   Schafer, *WDB,GS,* Vol. I, 49.

6.   *Ibid.,* 54-56.

7.   Copeland, "Cornish" and Schafer, *WDB,GS,* Vol. I, 49-57 and all of Vol. III.

8.   Robert C. Nesbit, *Wisconsin, A History* (Madison, 1973), 115.

9.   The most complete study of the Irish in Wisconsin is Sister M. Justille McDonald's published Ph.D. thesis from Catholic University, *History of the Irish in Wisconsin in the Nineteenth Century* (Washington, 1954). See also Schafer, *WDB,GS,* all vols. and Conzen, *Immigrant Milwaukee.*

10.   Schafer, *WDB,GS,* Vol. I, Fig. 13 and Conzen, Table 26, 129.

11.   The specific figures for total population and occupations come from McDonald, 51-53.

12.   Conzen argued, however, that the Irish community was not a complete one because it lacked a number of people in crucial occupations and thus had to turn to the rest of the city's population for certain services.

134   NOTES

13. Schafer, *WDB,GS,* Vol. I, Fig. 13.

14. John A. Hawgood, *The Tragedy of German-America, The Germans in the United States of America during the Nineteenth Century and After* (New York, 1940); Joseph Schafer, "The Yankee and the Teuton in Wisconsin," series in *WMH,* Vol. 6: 125-279, 386-402 and Vol. 7: 148-171; Kate A. Everest, "Early Lutheran Immigration to Wisconsin," *Transactions of the Wisconsin Academy of Sciences, Arts and Letters,* 8 (Madison, 1892), 289-298; Kate A. Everest Levi, "How Wisconsin Came By Its Large German Element," *Cols.* 12 (Madison, 1892), 299-334; Levi, "Geographical Origin of German Immigration to Wisconsin," *Cols.* 54 (Madison, 1898), 341-393; J. H. A. Lacher, "The German Element in Wisconsin," in Quaife, *Wisconsin,* Vol. II, 153-206; Guy-Harold Smith, "Notes on the Distribution of the German-born in Wisconsin," *WMH* 13 (December 1929), 107-120; Schafer, *WDB,GS,* all vols.; and Lieselotte Clemens, *Old Lutheran Emigration from Pomerania to the U.S.A.* (Hamburg, West Germany, 1976).

15. Levi, "Geographical Origin," 343-351.

16. Levi, "How," 302.

17. Schafer, *WDB,GS,* Vol. I, Fig. 13.

18. Rev. H. A. Muehlmeier, on behalf of Benjamin S. Stern, to the State Historical Society of Wisconsin, cited hereafter as SHSW, April 21, 1890, John S. Roeseler Papers, Box 1, cited hereafter as the Roeseler Papers, SHSW; *Geschichte Des Missionshauses in Belehrender und Erbaulicher Weise Zusammengestellt fur die Feier Seines Funfundzwanzigjahrigen Bestehens, 1885* (Cleveland, 1885); and Jerone C. Arpke, *Das Lippe Detmolder Settlement in Wisconsin* (Milwaukee, 1895). See also John E. Thomas, "Pioneer Settlement of Sheboygan County," *Cols.* 9 (1880-82), 389-396; Carl Ziller, ed., *History of Sheboygan County, Wisconsin, Past and Present* (Chicago, 1912); and Gustav Buchen, *Historic Sheboygan County* (Sheboygan, Wis., 1944).

19. Muehlmeier, *ibid.*

20. *Ibid.*

21. *Ibid.* Conzen found a similar situation in the much larger group of Germans in Milwaukee.

22. Albert O. Barton, "The Scandinavian Element in Wisconsin," in Quaife, *Wisconsin,* Vol. II, 107-152; Kendric D. Babcock, *The Scandinavian Element in the United States* (Urbana, Ill., 1912); and Guy-Harold Smith, "Notes on the Distribution of the Foreign-Born Scandinavians in Wisconsin in 1905," *WMH* 14 (June 1931), 419-436. See also Carlton C. Qualey, *Norwegian Settlement in the United States* (Northfield, Minn., 1938), 40-75; Ingrid Gaustad Semmingsen, "Norwegian Emigration to America During the Nineteenth Century," *Norwegian-American Studies and Records* 11 (Northfield, Minn., 1940), 66-81; Peter A. Munch, "Segregation and Assimilation of Norwegian Settlements in Wisconsin," *ibid.,* 18 (1954), 102-140; Oalf M. Norlie, *History of the Norwegian People in America* (Minneapolis, 1925).

23. E. T. Johnson to John S. Roeseler, November 29, 1888, Roeseler Papers. See also Malcolm L. Rosholt, *Our County, Our Story: Portage County, Wisconsin* (Portage, 1959); and Edward McGlochlin *et al,* eds., *A Standard History of Portage County* (Chicago, 1919).

24. Johnson, *ibid.*

25. John Luchsinger, "The Swiss Colony in New Glarus," *Cols.* 8 (Madison, 1879), 411-439; and Luchsinger, "The Planting of the Swiss Colony at New Glarus, Wisconsin," *Cols.* 12 (1892), 335-382. See also John Paul von Grueningen, ed., *The Swiss in the United States* (Madison, 1940), 31-34.

26. Babcock, *Scandinavian,* 53. See also Adolph B. Benson and Naboth Hedin, *Americans from Sweden* (Philadelphia, 1950).

27. T. Benoit to Reuben G. Thwaites, March 18, 1889, Roeseler Papers. See also *Ashland and Washburn, Wisconsin, Illustrated* (Milwaukee, 1891) and *Ashland and Environs* (Neenah, Wis., 1888).

28. Thomas P. Christensen, "Danish Settlement in Wisconsin," *WMH* 12 (September 1928), 19-40.

29. John D. Buenker, "Immigration and Ethnicity," in Nicholas C. Burckel, ed., *Racine: Growth and Change in a Wisconsin County* (Racine, 1977).

30. *Ibid.*, 26.

31. *Ibid.*, 3.

32. *Ibid.*, 12.

33. *Ibid.*, 11.

34. *Ibid.*, 16.

35. See Arnold Mulder, *Americans from Holland* (Philadelphia, 1947); Henry S. Lucas, "The First Dutch Settlers in Milwaukee," *WMH* 30 (December 1946), 174-183; Xavier Martin, "Belgians of Northeastern Wisconsin," *Pro.* 13 (Madison, 1895), 375-396; John I. Kolehmainen and George W. Hill, *Haven in the Woods: The Story of the Finns in Wisconsin* (Madison, 1951); Harry K. White, "The Icelanders on Washington Island," *Cols.* 54 (Madison, 1898), 335-340; and Conan B. Eaton, "The Icelanders in Wisconsin," *WMH* 56 (Autumn 1972), 3-20.

36. John W. S. Tomkiewicz, "Polanders in Wisconsin," *Pro.* (Madison, 1901), 148-152.

37. Thaddeus Borum, *We the Milwaukee Poles* (Milwaukee, 1946); Anthony J. Kuzniewski, "Milwaukee's Poles, 1866-1918; The Rise and Fall of a Model Community," *Milwaukee History* 1 (Spring and Summer 1978), 13-24; Donald E. Pienkos, "Politics, Religion and Change in Polish Milwaukee, 1900-1930," *WMH* 61 (Spring 1978), 179-209; Gwen Schultz, "Evolution of the Areal Patterns of German and Polish Settlement in Milwaukee," *Erdkunde* 10 (1956), 136-140; Laura Sutherland, "The Immigrant Family in the City: Milwaukee's Poles, 1880-1905," unpublished M.A. thesis, University of Wisconsin-Milwaukee, 1974; and Joseph A. Litzow, "Poles in Milwaukee, 1906-1909," unpublished M.A. thesis, St. Francis Seminary, Milwaukee, 1944.

38. The information on the Poles in Manitowoc originated in an essay probably penned by Roeseler, but based on information obtained from a Manitowoc Polish priest by Jacob Fliegler, *circa* 1890, Roeseler Papers. See also Paul E. Strub, "The Rise of Industrial Manitowoc, Wisconsin," B.A. thesis, University of Wisconsin, Madison, 1931; and the Manitowoc County Centennial Committee, *Story of a Century, Manitowoc County During Wisconsin's First Hundred Years, 1848-1948* (Manitowoc, 1948).

39. J. J. Vlach, "Our Bohemian Population," *Pro.* (Madison, 1901), 159-162; and Karel D. Bicha, "The Czechs in Wisconsin History," *WMH* 53 (Spring 1970), 194-203.

40. The information on the Bohemians in Kewaunee County originated in an essay probably written by Roeseler, *circa* 1890, Roeseler Papers.

41. *Ibid.*

42. See note 1 and Salvatore J. Tagliavia, "Italians in Milwaukee," unpublished M.A. thesis, St. Francis Seminary, 1946; Alberto C. Meloni, "Italy Invades the Bloody Third: The Early History of Milwaukee's Italians," *Historical Messenger of the Milwaukee County Historical Society* 25 (March 1969), 34-35; and Louis J. Swichkow and Lloyd P. Gartner, *A History of the Jews of Milwaukee* (Philadelphia, 1963). Surprisingly little has appeared on the non-Jewish Russians, Austrians, and Hungarians in Wisconsin. The best manuscript collection for these groups is the Roeseler Papers.

43. Marie Prisland, "The Slovenians, Most Recent American Immigrants," *WMH* 33

(March 1950), 265-280. See also Theodore Salutos, "The Greeks of Milwaukee," *WMH* 53 (Spring 1970), 175-193.

44. The information on the Russian Catholic Colony in Milwaukee originated in an essay written by Roeseler, *circa* 1890, Roeseler Papers.

45. *Ibid.*

46. *Ibid.*

47. An explanation of the computation procedures for Table 1.4 is in Karl E. and Alma F. Taeuber, *Negroes in Cities: Residential Segregation and Neighborhood Change* (Chicago, 1965), 28-31, 235-238.

48. Unfortunately all measures of geographic segregation suffer in that groups often cluster within single counties and that sometimes these clusters sit astride county boundaries. In the case of Wisconsin's immigrants, as Map 2 illustrates, small intracounty clusters go undetected while other clusters disappear statistically because county lines dissect them. The county-level indexes, based on the only tabulated data available, therefore, must surely understate first-generation segregation in the state. These first-generation immigrant indexes, therefore, serve as only rough guidelines to the more subtle residential segregation that was present, but numerically elusive. This problem is analytically akin to the "ecological fallacy" discussed in a continuing series of articles in the *Journal of Interdisciplinary History:* E. Terrence Jones, "Ecological Inference and Electorial Analysis," 2 (Autumn 1972), 249-262; J. Morgan Kousser, "Ecological Regression and the Analysis of Past Politics," 4 (Autumn 1973), 237-262; Allan J. Lichtman, "Correlation, Regression, and the Ecological Fallacy," 3 (Winter 1974), 417-433; and Jones, "Using Ecological Regression," 4 (Spring 1974), 593-596.

49. In this case, foreign-born rather than first-generation and second-generation figures appear because the purpose is to illustrate the imbalance in the sex ratios caused by the relative influx of males. Second-generation members arrive by birth, not physical movement, so the sex ratios for them would naturally have been more nearly balanced. It is impossible to separate them from the native-born in this instance because of the peculiar census tabulation for the topic.

50. Jack E. Eblen, "An Analysis of the Nineteenth-Century Frontier Populations," *Demography* 2 (1965), 399-413. Eblen's central point, however, was that the embalance of sex ratios on the frontier has been overstated.

51. See Chapter 3.

52. This sample and the one from the 1880 U.S. Census are the ones described in notes 11-12 of the introduction.

53. For an introduction to this work, see Tamara K. Hareven, "The Historical Study of the Family Cycle," *The Family in Historical Perspective Newsletter,* Series II (Spring 1974), 12-13.

54. The farms of the Eastern Europeans were often small and of less value than others. See Arlan Helgeson, *Farms in the Cutover: Agri-Settlement in Northern Wisconsin* (Madison, 1962).

55. With the exceptions indicated below, the religious information comes from the previously noted sources on individual immigrant groups.

56. U.S. Censuses as listed in note 1.

57. Levi, "Geographical Origin." The Protestant majority was much greater in Bavaria than in Baden.

58. The statement is based on estimates made from the U.S. Censuses of 1906 (religious) and 1910, with the assumption that the relationship between the numbers of German-born and German Protestant (or Catholic) individuals roughly equals that of the

number of all individuals born in largely Protestant (or Catholic) countries and the total
of Protestants (or Catholics). For the religious data, see U.S. Census, *Religious Bodies:
1906,* Part I (Washington, 1919), Table 4, 371-373.

59.   The basis for the decision to classify all people with Irish backgrounds as Catholic
is the research by Sister M. Justille McDonald, *History,* who presented (pp. 194-224)
church estimates of the numbers of Irish and German Catholics that left little room for
non-Catholics in the Irish population. She in addition had counted the number of Protestant Irish clergyman in the 1850 and 1860 U.S. census manuscripts and reported (pp.
224-225) finding only 11 and 15, respectively. She further speculated that even those
small numbers probably included several itinerant missionaries, especially among the
Baptists and Methodists, who together comprised 12 of the 26 total ministers.

60.   This figure represents the division of the 1916 Jewish total by the interpolated
Russian population for that year. U.S. Census, *Religious Bodies: 1916,* Part I (Washington, 1919), Table 63, 327-328. According to Niles Carpenter, *Immigrants and Their
Children, 1920: A Study Based on Census Statistics Relative to the Foreign Born and th
the Native White of Foreign or Mixed Parentage, Census Monographs,* VII (Washington,
1927), Table 165, 364-367 and Table 169, 376-384, only 2.2% of the foreign-born in the
state and 6.0% in Milwaukee spoke Hebrew or Yiddish. See also Swichkow and Gartner,
History.

61.   Other bits of background information about Wisconsin's immigrants would be
useful as well. For example, this analysis would gain from material on the family structures and familial roles of the immigrants. Such information might provide keys to
understanding the function of familial pressures on individual decision-making. Similarly,
a knowledge of the average incomes or amounts of wealth accumulated by immigrant
group members might add insight to the role of status in the process of assimilation. Evidence as to the ability of the immigrants to speak English or their rates of naturalization
by the number of years in the United States would supply hints about their groups'
ability to interact with outsiders. Unfortunately, no statewide tabulations are available
on such topics so it is necessary to analyze the characteristics of the immigrants from the
information available.

62.   This research will hereafter analyze the two major groupings separately so as to
better understand the differences among nationality groups. Since the number of groups
makes intense separate study difficult, examination of the major groupings seem pre-
ferable to the alternative of a simple immigrant/nonimmigrant dichotomy.

Chapter 2: Intermarriage Rates

1.   See Gretchen E. Kletzien's "Early History of New Holstein," in The New Holstein Centenniel, Inc., *New Holstein Centenniel Souvenir Booklet* (New Holstein, Wis.,
1948).

2.   Severin to Rueben G. Thwaites, March 15, 1889, John S. Roeseler Papers, Box
1, cited hereafter as the Roeseler Papers, State Historical Society of Wisconsin, Madison.
In nineteenth-century Wisconsin, the term "Yankee" referred to any native-born person
from east of Chicago.

3.   Fuehr to either Roeseler or Thwaites, August 17, 1888, Roeseler Papers.

4.   The data used in this chapter include all persons whom the 1850-1880 U.S.
Censuses recorded as married within the previous year and living with their spouses, and
systematic samples from the state marriage registrations of one-third for 1890-1910 and
one-half for 1920, ranging from nearly 5,000 to over 11,000 in size. The Canadians

illustrate one of the limitations on these data sets. The Canadian population was not homogeneous. It contained the members of many ethnic groups (most importantly the English- and French-speaking subpopulations), thus it is difficult to ethnically define a "Canadian." The problem recurs with Russians, Austrians, and, to a lesser extent, all of the groups. Both the censuses and marriage records used here record only birthplace, not cultural heritage.

5. Small sample sizes account for the termination of the Irish curve in 1900 and in later graphs the initiation of the Russian curves in that year.

6. The German decline from 1880 to 1890 may be more an artifact of changing data sets than a real increase.

7. The next largest Eastern European group, the Hungarians, was too small for use in this analysis.

8. Since only four Hungarian-Americans were in the sample for 1910, they were excluded from further analysis.

9. The 1850 and 1860 censuses asked no questions about parentage while the 1870 census determined only whether parents were natives of the United States or were foreign-born. Of the years included here, only 1910 fell within the period when the marriage records included parents' birthplaces.

10. For studies recognizing the importance of rural-urban location differentials, see Niles Carpenter, *Immigrants and Their Children, 1920: A Study Based on Census Statistics Relative to the Foreign Born and the Native White of Foreign or Mixed Parentage, Census Monographs,* VII (Washington, 1927); Simon Marcson, "A Theory of Intermarriage and Assimilation," *Social Forces* 29 (October 1950), 75-78; and Bengt Ankarloo, "Marriage," an unpublished paper presented to the MSSB Conference, Williams College, July 20-28, 1975, 26pp.

11. The added cost of separating the small number of 1880 and 1910 Milwaukee County residents who lived outside the city led to the use of county rather than city tallies. Labeling these people "urban" should have only a small effect on the findings, however, for only 16.6% in 1880 and 13.7% in 1910 lived in the county but not the city. Moreover, in 1910, only 2.5% of the total county population lived in civil divisions smaller than 2,500 people.

12. There is no previous work on intermarriage in Milwaukee. Joseph Schafer in his famous *Wisconsin Domesday Book, General Studies,* Vol. II: *Four Wisconsin Counties: Prairie and Forest* (Madison, Wis., 1927), 182, did cite a University of Wisconsin M.S. thesis by Arthur Henry Moeck entitled "Intermarriage in Milwaukee," 1922, but the university has no record of this work. There is, however, a record of an entirely different thesis completed by Moeck several years later.

13. Some 68.2% of the first generation and 77.0% of the second among the Western immigrants married outside Milwaukee County. Among the Eastern Europeans, over 60% of the first generation married within the county, but 74.7% of the second married outside. However, the second generation represented only a third of the Eastern European total.

14. The study suffers, as do all previous ones of its genre, from an inability to separate marriages contracted freely by the individuals themselves from those arranged by their parents or other relatives. Such distinctions might be feasible in localized case studies involving only a handful of marriers, but they are clearly beyond possibility for a broad-scale analysis. Thus, some distortions may appear in cases meeting two criteria: (1) individual marriers were markedly different from their own parents; (2) their parents were responsible for contracting the children's marriages. It seems unlikely, however, that both these specifications were met in very many of the cases.

Chapter 3: Individual Factors

1. U.S. Department of Commerce and Labor, Division of Naturalization, Naturalization Records, Racine Series 46, 1838-1964 (Manuscripts), Archives and Area Research Center, University of Wisconsin-Parkside, Kenosha, no pagination; and Wisconsin Marriage Records, 1900.

2. Racine City Directory, 1899.

3. *A Standard History of Sauk County,* Vol. II (Chicago, 1918), 769-771. For methodological comments on "mug books" such as this, see Archibald Hanna, "Every Man His Own Biographer," *Proceedings of the American Antiquarian Society* 80 (1970), 291-198.

4. *Sauk County,* 770.

5. Interview with Addie Hickman Scheffler, Milwaukee, June 27, 1978.

6. *Ibid.*

7. Interview with Paul R. Pace, née Poczoch, Milwaukee, June 26, 1978, and manuscript marriage registration records for Milwaukee County, No. 262-456, 1916, County Courthouse, Milwaukee.

8. Total independence of the individual's characteristics from those of potential spouses is not possible. For example, the forthcoming contention that Protestants married across nationality lines more than Catholics was due in part to the larger number of potential Protestant out-group mates for all, or nearly all, marriers.

9. Julius Drachsler, *Democracy and Assimilation: The Blending of Immigrant Heritages in America* (New York, 1920); and Milton L. Barron, ed., *The Blending American: Patterns of Intermarriage* (Chicago, 1972).

10. June 28, 1948, no page number given.

11. James Bossard, "Nationality and Nativity as Factors in Marriage," *American Sociological Review,* cited hereafter as *ASR,* 4 (December 1939), 792-798; and John L. Thomas, "The Factor of Religion in the Selection of Marriage Mates," *ASR* 16 (August 1951), 487-491.

12. John Burma, "Interethnic Marriage in Los Angeles, 1948-1959," *Social Forces* 42 (December 1963), 156-165.

13. Barron, *Blending,* 43.

14. Burma, "Interethnic." The same did not hold true, however, for the whites in Burma's sample group. See also Robert Schoen *et al,* "Intermarriage Among Spanish Surnamed Californians, 1962-1874," *International Migration Review* 12 (Fall 1978), 359-369.

15. Barron, *Blending,* 43.

16. Drachsler, *Democracy,* 147-148.

17. *Ibid.;* August B. Hollingshead, "Cultural Factors in the Selection of Marriage Mates," *ASR* 15 (October 1950), 619-627; Ulf Beijobom, *Swedes in Chicago: A Demographic and Social Study of the 1846-1880 Immigration* (Uppsala, Sweden, 1971).

18. The argument should run deeper, for immigrants and natives hardly had the same opportunities for out-marriage within the upper class. The native-born dominated the upper ranks of society, thus creating the type of group size problem analyzed in Chapter 4.

19. Niles Carpenter, *Immigrants and Their Children, 1920: A Study Based on Census Statistics Relative to the Foreign-Born and the Native White of Foreign or Mixed Parentage, Census Monographs,* VII (Washington, 1927), 246-247, and Paul C. Glick, "Intermarriage Among Ethnic Groups in the United States," *Social Biology* 17 December 1970), 297.

P. 77

20. Konrad Bercovici, *On New Shores* (New York, 1925), 37.

21. John Hawgood, *The Tragedy of German-America, The Germans in the United States of America during the Nineteenth Century and After* (New York, 1940); and Carpenter, *Immigrants*.

22. Some elements in this model are largely self-evident. Out-marriage is marriage across nationality lines. First-generation status goes to those who actually migrated to the United States and second-generation to their children born here. A person's age is a matter of years. Prior marriage is dichotomous: yes is a value of one, no is zero.

The other parts of the model require surrogates, measurable features that represent the actual traits under analysis. The size of a person's community was the rank of his or her place of marriage on a four-point scale. The categories, constituting separate dichotomous variables, are Milwaukee, medium-sized cities (25,000 to 100,000), small cities and towns (2,500 to 25,000), and rural areas of less than 2,500. Origins in lands dominated by particular religious groups (Protestant, Catholic, or Other and Unknown) or linguistic groups (English, Teutonic, Scandinavian, Slavic, or Romance) represent the individual's own religious or linguistic background.

Ruby Jo Reeves Kennedy, "Marriage in New Haven Since 1870, Statistically Analyzed and Culturally Interpreted," unpublished Ph.D. thesis, Yale University, 1938; "Single or Triple Melting Pot? Intermarriage Trends in New Haven, 1870-1940," *American Journal of Sociology*, cited hereafter as *AJS*, 49 (January 1944), 331-339; "Single or Triple Melting-Pot? Intermarriage in New Haven, 1870-1950," *AJS* 58 (July 1952), 56-59; and Hollingshead, "Cultural Factors" are the main advocates of determining religion on the basis of country of birth. There are problems with such indicators, however, especially in the cases of Canadians and Germans. Since their homelands contain sizable numbers of both Protestants and Catholics, it is necessary to know an immigrant's particular birthplace (province or state) to determine his religious heritage. Unfortunately, the early censuses and later marriage records rarely reported the subdivisions where the Canadians were born, thus forcing these people into the unknown category for religion. With some difficulty, however, it is possible to divide the Germans according to religion on the basis of birthplace and residence in Wisconsin. Presumably, natives of Bavaria and Baden were Catholics while Prussians divided between the Catholic and Protestant faiths. Other Germans were probably Protestants, at least nominally. Unfortunately, the marriage records were quite inconsistent in listing the specific German states of birth. Kate A. Everest, "How Wisconsin Came by its Large German Element," *Collections of the State Historical Society of Wisconsin* 12 (Madison, 1892), 299-334, did, however, indicate the areas of the state settled by immigrants from particular German subregions, and John S. Roeseler's survey of Wisconsin's immigrant communities had the same effect. Thus, the Everest and Roeseler materials (i.e., the Roeseler Papers at the State Historical Society of Wisconsin, Madison) serve as indicators of the German state of origin, and presumably the dominant religion, of the people of given Wisconsin communities, including the individuals in question.

As for the others among the Western immigrants, it was assumed that all but the Irish and French (both Catholic) and the Belgians (mixed and therefore unknown) were Protestants. The Eastern European immigrants appear as Catholics, despite a number of freethinkers (especially Czechs) among them. See Karel D. Bicha, "The Czechs in Wisconsin History," *Wisconsin Magazine of History* 53 (Spring 1970), 194-203. As noted in Chapter 2, Jews were too few in number to be included in such an analysis. All whose religions remained unknown fell from the analysis.

Language indicators posed similar problems. At the state-wide level, it is difficult to know the language of Canadians and Bohemians. Some one-fourth of the 1910 Canadians in Wisconsin, for example, probably spoke French as their first language since they were born in the French-speaking provinces. All Canadians appear here as English-speaking, however, on the assumption that most of the minority used English as a second language. Bicha, however, suggests that the main Bohemian migration into Wisconsin originated from Slavic areas. By 1910, 44,000 persons in Wisconsin who spoke Czech as their first language merit the listing of Bohemians under the Slavic language group. U.S. Census, 1920, Vol. II: *Population* (Washington, 1922), Table 10, pp. 707-726, and Table 7, pp. 982-985.

The occupational classes are those of Stephan Thernstrom, *The Other Bostonians: Poverty and Progress in the American Metropolis, 1880-1970* (Cambridge, Mass., 1973), Appendix B, 289-304: Upper-level occupations include major proprietors and professionals; upper-middle positions are those held by minor proprietors, semiprofessionals, and clerks; middle occupations are skilled positions; lower-middle and lower occupations are those of semiskilled or unskilled workers. Two occupational categories do not actually denote status, thus the reason for treating these levels as dichotomous variables — farmers, including farm laborers, and those with no occupations given.

23. Stuart M. Blumin, in Appendix B, 227-238, of *The Urban Threshold, Growth and Change in a Nineteenth-Century American Community* (Chicago, 1976), argues against multiple regression analysis in cases such as this that use dichotomous variables. He instead adopted the log-linear modeling techniques of Yvonne M. Bishop, Stephen E. Fienberg, and Paul W. Holland, *Discrete Multivariate Analysis: Theory and Practice* (Cambridge, Mass., 1975). David Knoke, "A Comparison of Log-Linear and Regression Models for Systems of Dichotomous Variables," *Sociological Methods and Research* 3 (May 1975), 416-434, however, demonstrated that, "in instances where the dependent dichotomy falls in the range of .25 to .75 . . . the choice of method will probably make little difference since the results are likely to be identical (p. 432)." Since all of the out-marriage rates under consideration here meet this criteria, this study employs the more familiar multiple regression analysis.

24. In the first runs, 11 different groupings of the cases appeared. The groups included: all individuals, males, females, native-stock Americans, and Western and Eastern European immigrants. In this phase, the runs that included all marriers disguised important differences between the nativity groups, and thus they were not continued. The male and female runs, on the other hand, showed few differences in the factors affecting the sexes' out-marriage rates, thereby neutralizing the analytical value of their separate groupings. They too were omitted from later runs.

In some cases, the variables employed in the analysis-reflect the limits on data availability. For example, no information is available in the marriage records on literacy. In other cases, some variables are simply inappropriate for certain models. Thus, the native-stock models, for example, delete the generation factor.

The second phase of the analysis involved the stepwise elimination of all independent variables that added only marginally (less than .005) to the Multiple R^2, including those that correlated highly with other independent ones. When such correlations appeared, the variable having the lesser impact on intermarriage was eliminated.

25. Milton Gordon, *Assimilation in American Life: The Role of Race, Religion and National Origin* (New York, 1964). See the introduction of this study.

26. The cases in these regressions are subsets of the 1910 statewide sample. The variables are as described in note 22 above, except that religion and community size variables were excluded.

27. See note 22.

28. The collection and processing of this massive amount of data would not have been possible without the help of the National Science Foundation and Professor John D. Buenker and his students at the University of Wisconsin-Parkside. James C. Schneider and Anthony C. Polvino, both then of the University of Wisconsin, Madison, worked under a National Science Foundation grant and collected information on individuals from city directories and census manuscripts and naturalization records. Professor Buenker personally canvassed the marriage records of the Catholic churches of Racine. His students traced the names of marriers into that city's directories and tax assessment rolls.

29. These new, local-level variables are as follows: (1) Religion, a dichotomous variable based on the listing of all marriages involving at least one Catholic recorded in local parish records; (2) occupation, a series of dichotomous measures, grouped according to the scheme used for the statewide occupation variables with the following modifications: (a) a man's occupational status was his own unless he was under 30 years of age and his father was present in Racine, in which case his occupational rank became that of his father, and (b) a female's level was also her own unless her father was present, in which case, regardless of her age, she too assumed her father's rank; (3) home ownership, also a dichotomous variable, indicating whether or not a person or his parents owned the house in which they lived; and (4) the value of that home, a continuous variable.

30. U.S. Census, 1910, Vol. III: *Population* (Washington, 1913), Table II, p. 1096.

31. Wisconsin Bureau of Labor, *Tenth Biennial Report, 1900-1901* (Madison, 1902), 319-320.

Chapter 4: Group Factors

1. The author is grateful to John Sharpless of the University of Wisconsin and John Modell of the University of Minnesota for particularly useful comments on mate availability.

2. The best development of the "marriage market" concept is Charles Hirschman and Judah Matras, "A New Look at the Marriage Market and Nuptiality Rates, 1915-1958," *Demography* 8 (November, 1971), 549-569.

3. Marriage registrations of the state of Wisconsin (manuscripts), 1900, State Office Building, Madison, no pagination; and the city directories of Racine for 1897 (Racine Directory Co., no place or date of publication given) and 1899 (Frederick C. Bliss, Racine, no date or place of publication given).

4. *Ibid.*

5. Lowry Nelson, "Intermarriage Among Nationality Groups in a Rural Area of Minnesota," *American Journal of Sociology,* cited hereafter as AJS, 48 (March 1943), 585-592; Milton L. Barron, *People Who Intermarry, Intermarriage in a New England Industrial Community* (Syracuse, N.Y., 1946), 263; John S. Ellsworth, Jr., "The Relationship of Population Density to Residential Propinquity as a Factor in Marriage Selection," *American Sociological Review* 13 (August 1948), 444-448; and Lee G. Burchinal and Loren E. Chancellor, "Social Status, Religious Affiliation and Ages at Marriage," *Marriage and Family Life* 25 (May 1965), 219-221.

6. Paul H. Besanceney, "On Reporting Rates of Intermarriage," *AJS* 70 (May 1965), 718-719.

7. In this analysis, those who actually married serve as surrogates for those who were both eligible and willing to marry. This working assumption, a standard procedure

in the sociological literature, was first proved statistically viable by Niles Carpenter, *Immigrants and Their Children, 1920* . . . , U.S. Census Monograph VII (Washington, 1927), 233.

8. Stephen E. Fienberg was the first to encourage historians to use this method. See his article on the standardization of political data: "A Statistical Technic for Historians: Standardizing Tables of Counts," *Journal of Interdisciplinary History* 1 (Winter 1971), 305-315. The first to apply iterative rescaling to intermarriage data was Harry P. Travis, "Religious In-Marriage and Inter-Marriage in Canada, 1934-1969: A Methodological and Empirical Investigation," M.S. thesis, University of Wisconsin, Madison, 1973. For a concise explanation of iteration and its applications in social history, see Richard M. Bernard and John B. Sharpless, "Analyzing Structural Influence on Social History Data," *Historical Methods Newsletter*, cited hereafter as *HMN*, 11 (Summer 1978), 113-121.

9. Small sample sizes prevented the inclusion of additional groups.

10. Unfortunately, the iterative procedure prevents comparisons between sexes. Since the groups in the final, standardized table each contain 100 males and 100 females, the in-marrying percentage of both sexes is the same.

11. Here, too, small group sizes prevented the inclusion of additional groups.

12. Kingsley Davis, "Intermarriage in Caste Societies," *American Anthropologist* 43 (July-September 1941), 376-395. See also Ernest W. Burgess and Paul E. Wallin, "Homogamy in Social Characteristics," *AJS* 49 (September 1943), 109-124; Barron, *The Blending American: Patterns of Intermarriage* (Chicago, 1972), 101; and Simon Marcson, "A Theory of Intermarriage and Assimilation," *Social Forces* 29 (October 1950), 77. "Model" appears here in the sense discussed by J. Rogers Hollingsworth, "Some Problems in Theory Construction for Historical Analysis," *HMN* 7 (June 1974), 225-244. Hollingsworth wrote (p. 226) that a "model [as distinct from a theory] may specify the relations among a set of variables without attempting to state all the idealized environments to which it applies."

13. Since people of the same nationality tended to have the same religions and linguistic backgrounds, these variables operate only in relation to out-group mates. Age similarity is the negative absolute difference between an individual's own age and the mean age of the members of the opposite sex of his or her in- (or out-) group. The model employs the negative difference so that all of the predicted signs for individual/in-group relationships will be negative and those predicted for the individual/out-group ones will be positive. The other variables represent the percentages of a person's potential in- (or out-) group mates who share the same characteristic with the individual in question. To simplify analysis, only the strongest predictors among the many variables tested are reported here.

14. Religion, occupational levels, and home ownership variables all represent the percentages of potential in-group and out-group spouses with the same status as the person in question. Because of high correlations with home ownership, home value was excluded from these variable sets.

Chapter 5: The Melting Pot and the Altar: Conclusions

1. David Paul Thelen, *The Early Life of Robert M. La Follette, 1855-1884* (Chicago, 1966), 4-20.

2. *Ibid.,* 11-50.

3. Edward T. James, ed., *Notable American Women, 1607-1950: A Biographical Dictionary* (Cambridge, Mass., 1971), Vol. II, 356-367.

4. Belle Case La Follette and Fola La Follette, *Robert M. La Follette, June 14, 1855 - June 18, 1925* (New York, 1953), Vol. I, 32-33.

5. Thelen, *Early Life,* 42.

6. *Ibid.;* and Belle and Fola La Follette, *La Follette,* 53-54.

7. Belle and Fola La Follette, *ibid.* For a much more extensive treatment of La Follette and his politics in the context of progressivism, see Thelen, *Robert M. La Follette and the Insurgent Spirit* (Boston, 1976).

8. This in-group percentage, along with those following, originate in Chapter 2.

9. *History of Dane County: Biographical and Genealogical* (Madison, 1906), 387-388.

10. *Ibid.,* 291-292 and 488-489.

11. Marriage registrations of the state of Wisconsin (manuscripts), 1910, State Office Building, Madison, no pagination.

12. *Ibid.*

13. *Ibid.*

14. *Ibid.* Hailin's first name does not appear on the form.

15. As noted earlier, at the time of their marriage, Bob La Follette lived in Dane County, but his bride technically resided in neighboring Sauk County. Their case raises the methodological issue of defining residence, that is: Was residence at the time of marriage an adequate surrogate for residence during courtship? See Alvin M. Katz and Reuben Hill, "Residential Propinquity and Marital Selection: A Review of Theory, Method, and Fact," *Marriage and Family Living* 20 (February 1959), 27-35.

16. See Introduction.

Selected Bibliography

This bibliography brings together three types of materials—documentary, historical, and sociological—that relate directly to the study of intermarriage in Wisconsin. The documents include both published and unpublished items concerning that subject. Among these, the manuscript marriage records are the most valuable, especially those for 1907-1917 that list birthplaces of the couple's parents. Other unpublished documents offer additional information about particular persons. These include the United States and Wisconsin state censuses and the city directories, tax records, and naturalization records for Racine. The published materials are largely census documents, including special reports on marriage and divorce and the censuses of religious bodies, along with annual state reports on marriages filed by the Bureau of Labor and the Bureau of Vital Statistics.

The historical works focus on two topics, the history of the state of Wisconsin and the history of American immigration. The former category includes the major state histories, among which the emerging *History of Wisconsin* series sponsored by the State Historical Society is clearly the best. A projected set of six volumes, the series now includes the works of Alice E. Smith, *From Exploration to Statehood,* and Richard N. Current, *Wisconsin in the Civil War Era (1848-1873).* The best one-volume treatment of Wisconsin's history is Robert C. Nesbit's thoroughly enjoyable *Wisconsin, A History.* Other historical works cover Milwaukee, the best of which is clearly Bayrd Still's *Milwaukee,* and various other locales mentioned in the text. The category of immigration history includes only a few general works, such as John Higham's *Strangers in the Land,* centering instead on publications that specifically deal with Wisconsin's immigrants or that include specific information on such people as a part of broader treatments. The best of the former group is Kathleen Neils Conzen's *Immigrant Milwaukee.*

The sociological literature includes theoretical works, such as those discussed in the introduction, on mate selection and intermarriage across nationality lines in the United States. Any fundamental list of such publications should include Kingsley Davis, "Inter-

146   SELECTED BIBLIOGRAPHY

marriage in Caste Societies," *American Anthropoligist* (1941); Robert K. Merton, "Intermarriage and the Social Structure," *Psychiatry* (1941); Ruby Jo Reeves Kennedy, "Single or Triple Melting-Pot?" *American Journal of Sociology* (1944 and 1952); Milton Gordon, *Assimilation in American Life;* and C. A. Price and J. Zubrzycki, "The Use of Intermarriage Statistics as an Index of Assimilation," *Population Studies* (1962). The bibliography also includes case studies of marital assimilation ranging from the highly influential but flawed studies of Julius Drachsler, *Democracy and Assimilation,* Niles Carpenter, *Immigrants and Their Children, 1920,* and Kennedy, to the new frontier of intermarriage studies of Mexican-Americans, as represented by Edward Murguia and W. Parker Frisbie's "Trends in Mexican American Intermarriage: Recent Findings in Perspective," *Social Science Quarterly* (1977). Other sociological studies, both those on other types of intermarriage, for example, religious intermarriage, and on other topics not related to this subject, appear also if they demonstrate some methodological tool useful to the study of marital assimilation. For other works on marriage, see the Joan Aldous and Reuben Hill, eds., *International Bibliography of Research in Marriage and the Family, 1900-1964,* with supplements.

Governmental Documents

United States Government Published Documents

U.S. Census, *The Seventh Census of the United States: 1850*
   The Eighth Census of the United States: 1860
   The Ninth Census of the United States: 1870
U.S. Census Office, *The Tenth Census of the United States: 1880*
   The Eleventh Census of the United States: 1890
   The Twelfth Census of the United States: 1900
U.S. Bureau of the Census, *Religious Bodies: 1906*
   The Thirteenth Census of the United States: 1910
   Religious Bodies: 1916
   The Fourteenth Census of the United States: 1920
   Monographs, VII: Niles Carpenter, *Immigrants and Their Children, 1920: A Study Based on Census Statistics Relative to the Foreign Born and the Native White of Foreign or Mixed Parentage* (1927)
   Report on the Social Statistics of Cities (1887)
   Special Reports: Marriage and Divorce, 1867-1906 (1909)
   Marriage and Divorce, 1916 (1919)
   Marriage and Divorce, Annual Reports: 1923-1932 (1925-1934)
U.S. Department of Labor, *A Report on Marriage and Divorce in the United States, 1867 to 1886, Including an Appendix Relating to Marriage and Divorce in Certain Countries in Europe* (1889)

United States Government Unpublished Documents

U.S. Census Population Schedules, 1850-1880, 1900, Federal Records Center, Chicago, Illinois, microfilm
U.S. Department of Commerce and Labor, Division of Naturalization, Naturalization Records, Racine Series 46, 1838-1964, Archives and Area Research Center, University of Wisconsin-Parkside, Kenosha

Wisconsin State Government Published Documents

Wisconsin Bureau of Labor, *Tenth Biennial Report, 1900-1901* (Madison, 1902)
Wisconsin Bureau of Vital Statistics, *Biennial Reports,* in the *Biennial Reports* of the
State Board of Health, 1906-1920 (Madison)
Wisconsin State Census, *Tabular Statements of the Census Enumeration . . .* June 20,
1895 *(Madison, 1895)*
    Tabular Statements of the Census Enumeration . . . June 1, 1905

Wisconsin State Government Unpublished Documents

Wisconsin State Census Population Schedules, 1905, State Historical Society of Wisconsin, Madison
Wisconsin State Marriage Registrations, Wisconsin State Office Building, Madison

General Works

Aldous, Joan and Hill, Reuben, eds., *International Bibliography of Research in Marriage
    and the Family, 1900-1964,* with supplements, Minneapolis, 1967
Ander, Oscar F., ed., *The Trek of the Immigrants: Essays Presented to Carl Wittke,* Rock
    Island, Ill., 1964
Anderson, Rasmus B., *First Chapter of Norwegian Immigration, 1821-1840,* Madison,
    1895
Arpke, Jerone C., *Das Lippe-Detmolder Settlement in Wisconsin,* Milwaukee, 1895
Ashland and Environs, Neenah, Wis., 1888
Ashland and Washburn, Wisconsin, Illustrated, Milwaukee, 1891
Babcock, Kendric C., *The Scandinavian Element in the United States,* Urbana, Ill., 1912
Barron, Milton L., ed., *The Blending American: Patterns of Intermarriage,* Chicago, 1972
_____, *People Who Intermarry, Intermarriage in a New England Industrial Community,*
    Syracuse, N.Y., 1946
Barry, Coleman J., *The Catholic Church and German Americans, Catholic University of
    America Studies,* Vol. 40, Washington, 1953
Barton, Josef J., *Peasants and Strangers: Italians, Rumanians and Slovaks in an American
    City, 1890-1950,* Cambridge, Mass., 1975
Beijbom, Ulf, *Swedes in Chicago: A Demographic and Social Study of the 1846-1880
    Immigration,* Uppsala, Sweden, 1971
Benson, Adolph B., and Hedin, Naboth, *Americans from Sweden,* Philadelphia, 1950
Bercovici, Konrad, *On New Shores,* New York, 1925
Billington, Ray Allen, *The Protestant Crusade, 1800-1860: A Study of American Nativ-
    ism,* New York, 1938
Bishop, Yvonne M. M., Fienberg, Stephen E., and Holland, Paul W., *Discrete Multivariate
    Analysis: Theory and Practice,* Cambridge, Mass., 1975
Blegen, Theodore E., *Norwegian Migration to America, The American Transition,* North-
    field, Minn., 1940
Blied, Benjamin J., *The Catholic Story of Wisconsin,* Milwaukee, 1948
Blumin, Stuart M., *The Urban Threshold, Growth and Change in a Nineteenth-Century
    American Community,* Chicago, 1976
Borrie, W. D., *The Cultural Integration of Immigrants,* Paris, 1959
Borum, Thaddeus, *We the Milwaukee Poles,* Milwaukee. 1946
Bruce, William G., *A Short History of Milwaukee,* Milwaukee, 1936

148   SELECTED BIBLIOGRAPHY

———, *History of Milwaukee*, 3 vols., Chicago, 1922

Brunner, Edmund deS., *Immigrant Farmers and Their Children, With Four Studies of Immigrant Communities*, Garden City, N.Y., 1929

Buchen, Gustav, *Historic Sheboygan County*, Sheboygan, Wis., 1944

Burckel, Nicholas C., ed., *Racine: Growth and Change in a Wisconsin County*, Racine, Wis., 1977

Campbell, Henry C., *Wisconsin in Three Centuries, 1634-1905*, 5 vols., New York, 1906

Capek, Thomas, *The Cechs in America*, Boston, 1920

Carter, Hugh and Glick, Paul C., eds., *Marriage and Divorce: A Social and Economic Study*, Cambridge, Mass., 1970

Chudacoff, Howard P., *Mobile Americans: Residential and Social Mobility in Omaha, 1880-1920*, New York, 1972

Clemens, Lieselotte, *Old Lutheran Emigration from Pomerania to the U.S.A.*, Hamburg, West Germany, 1976

Conzen, Kathleen Neils, *Immigrant Milwaukee, 1836-1860: Accommodation and Community in a Frontier City*, Cambridge, Mass., 1976

Current, Richard N., *The History of Wisconsin, Vol. II: The Civil War Era, 1848-1873*, Madison, 1976

Curti, Merle, *The Making of an American Community: A Case Study of Democracy in a Frontier Community*, Stanford, Calif., 1959

de Crévecoeur, J. Hector St. Jean, *Letters from an American Farmer*, New York, 1904 edition

Drachsler, Julius, *Democracy and Assimilation: The Blending of Immigrant Heritages in America*, New York, 1920

Fairchild, H. P., *Immigrant Backgrounds*, New York, 1927

Geschichte Des Missionshauses in Belehrender und Erbaulicher Weise Zusammengestellt Für Die Feier Seines Funfundzwanzigjährigen Bestehens, 1885, Cleveland, 1885

Gilsdorf, Gordon, *Wisconsin's Catholic Heritage*, Madison, 1948

Goode, William, Hopkins, Elizabeth, and McClure, Helen M., *Social Systems and Family Patterns: A Propositional Inventory*, Indianapolis, 1971

Gordon, Albert I., *Intermarriage: Interfaith, Interracial, Interethnic*, Boson, 1964

Gordon, Milton, *Assimilation in American Life, The Role of Race, Religion, and National Origin*, New York, 1964

Gregory, John G., *History of Milwaukee, Wisconsin*, 4 vols., Chicago, 1931

———, *West Central Wisconsin: A History*, 4 vols., Indianapolis, 1933

Handlin, Oscar, *Boston's Immigrants: A Study in Acculturation*, Cambridge, Mass., 1941

Hawgood, John A., *The Tragedy of German-America, The Germans in the United States of America during the Nineteenth Century and After*, New York, 1940

Helgeson, Arlan, *Farms in the Cutover: Agri-Settlement in Northern Wisconsin*, Madison, 1962

Higham, John, *Strangers in the Land: Patterns of American Nativism, 1860-1925*, New Brunswick, N.J., 1955

History of Dane County: Biographical and Genealogical, Madison, 1906

Holand, Hjalmar R., *Wisconsin's Belgian Community*, Sturgeon Bay, Wis., 1933

Holmes, Fred L., *Old World Wisconsin: Around Europe in the Badger State*, Eau Claire, Wis., 1944

Hutchinson, E. P., *Immigrants and Their Children, 1850-1950*, New York, 1956

James, Edward T., ed., *Notable American Women, 1607-1950: A Biographical Dictionary*, Vol. II, Cambridge, Mass., 1971

Kleppner, Paul, *The Cross of Culture*, New York, 1970

Kolehmainen, John I., and Hill, George W., *Haven in the Woods: The Story of the Finns in Wisconsin,* Madison, 1951

Korman, A. Gerd, *Industrialization, Immigrants, and Americanizers: The View from Milwaukee, 1866-1021,* Madison, 1967

La Follette, Belle Case, and La Follette, Fola, *Robert M. La Follette, June 14, 1855-June 18, 1925,* New York, 1953

Leach, E. W., *History of the First Methodist Episcopal Church of Racine, Wisconsin,* Racine, 1912

———, *Racine, An Historical Narrative,* Racine, Wis., 1920

Lieberson, Stanley, *Ethnic Patterns in American Cities,* New York, 1963

Linder, Forrest E., and Grove, Robert D., *Vital Statistics Rates in the United States, 1900-1940,* Washington, 1943

Lucas, Henry S., *Netherlanders in America: Dutch Immigration to the United States and Canada, 1789-1950,* Ann Arbor, Mich., 1955

MacDonald, M. Justile, *History of the Irish in Wisconsin in the Nineteenth Century,* Washington, 1954

Manitowoc County Centennial Committee, *Story of a Century, Manitowoc County During Wisconsin's First Hundred Years, 1848-1948*

Marden, Charles F., and Meyer, Gladys, *Minorities in American Society,* New York, 1962

McGlochlin, Edward, *et al,* eds., *A Standard History of Portage County,* Chicago, 1919

Mulder, Arnold, *Americans from Holland,* Philadelphia, 1947

Nelli, Humbert S., *The Italians in Chicago, 1880-1930: A Study in Ethnic Mobility,* New York, 1970

Nelson, E. Clifford, and Fevold, Eugene L., *The Lutheran Church Among the Norwegian Americans,* 2 vols., Minneapolis, 1960

Nelson, O. N., ed., *History of the Scandinavians and Successful Scandinavians in the United States,* 2 vols., Minneapolis, 1893-97

Nesbit, Robert C., *Wisconsin, A History,* Madison, 1973

New Holstein Centennial, Inc., *New Holstein Centennial Souvenir Booklet,* New Holstein, Wis., 1948

Norlie, Olaf M., *History of the Norwegian People in America,* Minneapolis, 1925

Novak, Michael, *The Rise of the Unmeltable Ethnics: Politics and Culture in the Seventies* (New York, 1971)

O'Connor, Richard, *The German-Americans, An Informal History,* Boston, 1968

Portrait and Biographical Album of Racine and Kenosha Counties, Wisconsin, Chicago, 1892

Quaife, Milo M., *Wisconsin, Its History and Its People,* 4 vols., Chicago, 1924

Qualey, Carlton, C., *Norwegian Settlement in the United States,* Northfield, Minn., 1938

Rabb, Theodore K., and Rotberg, Robert I., eds. *The Family in History: Interdisciplinary Essays,* New York, 1971

Racine, Wisconsin, City Directories: 1883-4, 1897, 1899, 1901

Robertson, Wilmot, *The Dispossessed Majority,* Cape Canaveral, Fla., 1972

Rodman, Hyman, ed., *Marriage, Family and Society: A Reader,* New York, 1965

Rogoff, Natalie, *Recent Trends in Occupational Mobility,* Glencoe, Ill., 1953

Rosholt, Malcolm, L., *Our County, Our Store: Portage County, Wisconsin,* Portage, Wis., 1959

Saloutos, Theodore, *The Greeks in the United States,* Cambridge, Mass., 1964

Sankey, Alice, *Racine: The Belle City,* Racine, Wis., circa 1900

Schafer, Joseph, *Wisconsin Domesday Book, General Series:*
    Vol. I: *A History of Agriculture in Wisconsin,* Madison, 1922

150   SELECTED BIBLIOGRAPHY

Vol. II: *Four Wisconsin Counties: Prairie and Forest,* Madison, 1927
Vol. III: *The Wisconsin Lead Region,* Madison, 1932
Vol. IV: *The Winnebago-Horicon Basin,* Madison, 1932
———, *Wisconsin Domesday Book, Town Studies,* Vol I, Madison, 1924
Scheiber, Harry N., ed., *The Old Northwest: Studies in Regional History, 1789-1910,* Lincoln, Neb., 1968
Smith, Alice E., *The History of Wisconsin, Vol. I, From Exploration to Statehood,* Madison, 1973
Spengler, Joseph J., and Duncan, O. D., eds., *Demographic Analysis,* Glencoe, Ill, 1956
Still, Bayrd, *Milwaukee: The History of a City,* Madison, Wis., 1948
Stone, Fanny L., ed., *Racine, Belle City of the Lakes and Racine County, Wisconsin: A Record of Settlement, Organization, Progress and Achievement,* 2 vols., Chicago, 1916
✓ Swichkow, Louis J. and Lloyd P. Gartner, *A History of the Jews of Milwaukee,* Philadelphia, 1963
Taeuber, Karl E. and Alma F., *Negroes in Cities: Residential Segregation and Neighborhood Change,* Chicago, 1965
Thelen, David Paul, *Robert M. La Follette and the Insurgent Spirit,* Boston, 1976
———, *The Early Life of Robert M. La Follette, 1855-1884,* Chicago, 1966
Thernstrom, Stephan, *The Other Bostonians: Poverty and Progress in the American Metropolis, 1880-1970,* Cambridge, Mass., 1973
Thomas, William I., and Znaniecki, Florian, *The Polish Peasant in Europe and America, Monograph of an Immigrant Group,* 2 vols., New York, 1958
Vander Zanden, James W., *American Minority Relations,* New York, 1972
von Grueningen, John P., ed., *The Swiss in the United States,* Madison, 1940
Warner, Sam Bass, Jr. and Fleisch, Sylvia, *Measurements for Social History: Metropolitan America, 1860-1960,* Beverly Hills, Calif., 1977
Wessel, Bessie Bloom, *An Ethnic Survey of Woonsocket, Rhode Island,* Chicago, 1931
Williams, Daniel J., *One Hundred Years of Welsh Calvinistic Methodism in America,* Philadelphia, 1937
———, *The Welsh Community of Waukesha County* (Wis.), Columbus, Ohio, 1926
Wittke, Carl, *The German Language Press in America,* Lexington, Ky., 1957
———, *Refugees from Revolution: The German Forty-Eighters in America,* Philadelphia, 1952
Yans-McLaughlin, Virginia, *Family and Community: Italian Immigrants in Buffalo, 1880-1930,* Ithaca, New York, 1977
Ziller, Carl, ed., *History of Sheboygan County, Wisconsin, Past and Present,* Chicago, 1912

Articles

Abrams, Ray H., "Residential Propinquity as a Factor in Marriage Selection: Fifty Year Trends in Philadelphia," *American Sociological Review* 8 (June 1943), 288-294
Akers, Donald S., "On Measuring the Marriage Squeeze," *Demography* 4 (1967), 907-924
Aldridge, D. P., "Changing Nature of Interracial Marriage in Georgia: A Research Note," *Journal of Marriage and the Family* 35 (November 1973), 641-642
Banks, Franklin, Dintz, Simon, and Pasamanick, Benjamin, "Mate Selection and Social Class: Changes During the Past Quarter Century," *Marriage and Family Living* 21 (November 1969), 348-351
Barnett, Larry D., "Research in Interreligious Dating and Marriage," *Marriage and Family Living* 24 (May 1962), 191-194

Barron, Milton L., "The Incidence of Jewish Intermarriage in Europe and America," *American Sociological Review* 11 (January 1946), 6-13

Bean, Frank D., and Bradshaw, Benjamin S., "Intermarriage Between Persons of Spanish and Non-Spanish Surnames: Changes from the Mid-Nineteenth to the Mid-Twentieth Century," *Social Science Quarterly* 51 (September 1970), 389-395

Besenceney, Paul H., "On Reporting Rates of Intermarriage," *American Journal of Sociology* 70 (May 1965), 717-721

Bicha, Karel D., "The Czechs in Wisconsin History," *Wisconsin Magazine of History* 53 (Spring 1970), 194-203

Blegen, Theodore C., "The Competition of the Northwestern States for Immigrants," *Wisconsin Magazine of History* 3 (September 1919), 3-29

Bossard, James H. S., "Nationality and Nativity as Factors in Marriage," *American Sociological Review* 4 (December 1939), 792-798

_____, "Residential Propinquity as a Factor in Marriage Selection," *American Journal of Sociology* 28 (September 1932), 219-224

_____, and Letts, Harold C., "Mixed Marriages Involving Lutherans: A Research Report, *Marriage and Family Living* 18 (November 1956), 308-310

Bruncken, Ernest, "How Germans Became Americans," *Proceedings of the State Historical Society of Wisconsin, 1897* (1897), 101-122

Bryden, James A., "The Scots in Wisconsin," *Proceedings of the State Historical Society of Wisconsin, 1901* (1901), 153-158

Bumpass, Larry, "The Trend of Interfaith Marriage in the United States," *Social Biology* 17 (December 1970), 253-259

Burchinal, Lee G., "Membership Groups and Attitudes Toward Cross Religious Dating and Marriage," *Marriage and Family Living* 22 (August 1960), 248-253

_____, and Chancellor, Loren, E., "Ages at Marriage, Occupations of Grooms and Interreligious Marriage Rates," *Social Forces* 40 (May 1962), 348-354

_____, "Compilation of State and Diocese Reported Marriage Data for Iowa, 1953-57," *American Catholic Sociological Review* 23 (Spring 1962), 21-29

_____, "Social Status, Religious Affiliation and Ages at Marriage," *Marriage and Family Living* 25 (May 1963), 219-221

_____, "Survival Rates Among Religiously Homogamous and Interreligious Marriages," *Social Forces* 41 (May 1963), 353-362

Burgess, Ernest W., and Wallin, Paul, "Homogamy in Social Characteristics," *American Journal of Sociology* 49 (September 1943), 109-124

Burma, John H., "Interethnic Marriage in Los Angeles, 1948-1959," *Social Forces* 42 (December 1963), 156-165

Cabe, Patrick A., "Name Length as a Factor in Mate Selection," *Psychological Reports* 21 (April 1967), 678

Catton, William R., Jr., and Smircich, R. J., "A Comparison of Mathematical Modes for the Effect of Residential Propinquity on Mate Selection," *American Sociological Review* 29 (August 1964), 522-529

Chancellor, Loren E., and Burchinal, Lee G., "Relation among Interreligious Marriages, Migratory Marriages, and Civil Weddings in Iowa," *Eugenics Quarterly* 9 (June 1962), 75-83

_____, and Monahan, Thomas P., "Religious Preference and Interreligious Mixtures in Marriages and Divorces in Iowa," *American Journal of Sociology* 61 (November 1955), 233-239

_____, "Statistical Aspects of Marriage and Divorce by Religious Denomination in Iowa, *Eugenics Quarterly* 2 (September 1955), 162-173

Christensen, H. T. and Barber, K., "Interfaith vs. Intrafaith Marriage in Indiana," *Marriage and Family Living* 29 (August 1967), 461-469

Christensen, Thomas P., "Danish Settlement in Wisconsin," *Wisconsin Magazine of History* 12 (September 1928), 19-40

Chudacoff, Howard P., "A New Look at Ethnic Neighborhoods: Residential Dispersion and the Concept of Visibility in a Medium-Sized City," *Journal of American History* 60 (June 1973), 76-93

Clarke, Alfred C., "An Examination of the Operation of Residential Propinquity as a Factor in Mate Selection," *American Sociological Review* 17 (February 1952), 17-22

Coale, Ansley J., "Age Patterns of Marriage," *Population Studies* 25 (July 1971), 193-214

Cohen, Steven M., "Socioeconomic Determinants of Interethnic Marriage and Friendship," *Social Forces* 55 (June 1977), 997-1010

Cooper, Bernice, "Die Freien Geniwden in Wisconsin," *Transactions of the Wisconsin Academy of Sciences, Arts, and Letters* 53 (1964), 53-69

Copeland, Louis A., "The Cornish in Wisconsin," *Collections of the State Historical Society of Wisconsin* 14 (1898), 301-334

Cottrell, A. B., "Cross-national Marriage as an Extension of the International Life-Style: A Study of Indian-Western Couples," *Journal of Marriage and the Family* 35 (November 1973), 739-741

Davie, Maurice R. and Reeves, Ruby Jo, "Propinquity of Residence Before Marriage," *American Journal of Sociology* 44 (January 1939), 510-517

Davis, Kingsley, "Intermarriage in Caste Societies," *American Anthropologist* 43 (July-September 1941), 376-395

Davis, Moshe, "Mixed Marriages in Western Jewry, Historical Background to the Jewish Response," *Jewish Journal of Sociology* 10 (December 1968), 177-220

Dickie, Anna Adams, "Scotch-Irish Presbyterian Settlers in Southern Wisconsin," *Wisconsin Magazine of History* 31 (March 1948), 291-304

DiSanto, Joseph E., "Marital Status 1900-1960, and Marriage 1960, of Wisconsin's Population," *Population Series,* No. 7, Department of Rural Sociology, University of Wisconsin, Madison (November 1963)

Duncan, Otis D., with John H. McClure, James Salisbury, Jr., and Richard H. Simmons, "The Factor of Age in Marriage," *American Journal of Sociology* 39 (January 1934), 469-482

Eaton, Conan B., "The Icelanders in Wisconsin," *Wisconsin Magazine of History* 56 (Fall 1972), 2-20

Eblen, Jack E., "An Analysis of Nineteenth Century Frontier Populations," *Demography* 2 (1965), 399-413

Ecklund, Bruce K., "Theories of Mate Selection," *Eugenics Quarterly* 15 (June 1968), 71-84

Ellsworth, John S., Jr., "The Relationship of Population Density to Residential Propinquity as a Factor in Marriage Selection," *American Sociological Review* 13 (August 1948), 444-448

Feldman, Ephraim, "Intermarriage Historically Considered," *Yearbook of the Central Conference of American Rabbis* 19 (1909), 271-307

Fienberg, Stephen E., "A Statistical Technic for Historians: Standardizing Tables of Counts," *Journal of Interdisciplinary History* 1 (Winter 1971), 305-315

Fitzpatrick, Joseph P., "Intermarriage of Puerto Ricans in New York City," *American Journal of Sociology* 71 (January 1966), 395-406

Garrison, Robert J., Anderson, V. Elving, and Reed, Sheldon C., "Assortative Mating," *Eugenics Quarterly* 15 (June 1968), 113-127

Glick, Paul C., "First Marriages and Remarriages," *American Sociological Review* 14 (December 1949), 726-734

_____, "Intermarriage Among Ethnic Groups in the United States," *Social Biology* 17 (December 1970), 292-298

_____, "Intermarriage and Fertility Patterns Among Persons in Major Religious Groups," *Eugenics Quarterly* 7 (March 1960), 31-38

Gordon, Michael, and Bernstein, M. Charles, "Mate Choice and Domestic Life in the Nineteenth-Century Marriage Manual," *Journal of Marriage and the Family* 32 (November 1970), 665-674

Greeley, Andrew M., "Religious Intermarriage in a Denominational Society," *American Journal of Sociology* 75 (May 1970), 949-952

Gregory, John G., "Foreign Immigration to Wisconsin," *Proceedings of the State Historical Society of Wisconsin, 1901* (1902), 137-143

Gurak, Douglas T. and Kritz, Mary M., "Intermarriage Patterns in the U.S.: Maximizing Information from the U.S. Census Public Use Samples," *Review of Public Data Use* 6 (March 1978), 33-43

Hansen, Blaine, "The Norwegians of Luther Valley," *Wisconsin Magazine of History* 28 (June 1945), 422-430

Hareven, Tamara K., "The Historical Study of the Family Cycle," *The Family in Historical Perspective,* Series II (Spring 1974), 12-13

Harris, J. Arthur, "Assortative Mating in Man," *The Popular Science Monthly* 80 (May 1912), 476-492

Haugen, Einar, "Norwegian Migration to America," *Norwegian-American Studies and Records* 18 (1954), 1-23

Heer, David M., "Trend of Interfaith Marriages in Canada: 1922-57," *American Sociological Review* 27 (April 1962), 245-250

Heiss, J. S., "Interfaith Marriage and Marital Outcome," *Marriage and Family Living* 23 (August 1961), 228-233

_____, "Premarital Characteristics of the Religiously Intermarried in an Urban Area," *American Sociological Review* 25 (February 1960), 47-55

Hense-Hensen, Wilhelm, "Influence of the Germans in Wisconsin," *Proceedings of the State Historical Society of Wisconsin, 1901* (1901), 144-147

Hirschman, Charles, and Matras, Judah, "A New Look at the Marriage Market and Nuptiality Rates, 1915-1958," *Demography* 8 (November 1971), 549-569

Hollingshead, August B., "Age Relationships and Marriage," *American Sociological Review* 16 (August 1951), 492-499

_____, "Cultural Factors in the Selection of Marriage Mates," *American Sociological Review* 15 (October 1950), 619-627

Hollingsworth, J. Rogers, "Some Problems in Theory Construction for Historical Analysis," *Historical Methods Newsletter* 7 (June 1974), 225-244

Hunt, Thomas C., "Occupational Status and Marriage," *American Sociological Review* 5 (August 1940), 495-504

Johnson, Hildegard Binder, "Intermarriage Between German Pioneers and Other Nationalities in Minnesota in 1860 and 1870," *American Journal of Sociology* 51 (January 1946), 299-304

Jones, E. Terrence, "Ecological Inference and Electoral Analysis," *Journal of Interdisciplinary History* 2 (Autumn 1972), 249-262

Jarstad, "The melting pot in Northeastern Wisconsin"
WMH., 26 (1943) 426-432.

———, "Using Ecological Regression," *Journal of Interdisciplinary History* 4 (Spring 1974), 593-596

Karp, Ellen S., Jackson, Julie H., and Lester, David, "Ideal-Self Fulfillment in Mate Selection: A Corollary to the Complementary Need Theory of Mate Selection," *Journal of Marriage and the Family* 32 (May 1970), 269-272

Katz, Alvin M., and Hill, Reuben, "Residential Propinquity and Marital Selection: A Review of Theory, Method, and Fact," *Marriage and Family Living* 20 (February 1958), 27-35

Kemper, Theodore D., "Mate Selection and Marital Satisfaction According to Sibling Type of Husband and Wife," *Journal of Marriage and the Family* 28 (August 1966), 346-349

Kendel, William F., Himler, Joyce and Cole, Leonard, "Religious Socialization, Present Devoutness, and Willingness to Enter a Mixed Religious Marriage," *Sociological Analysis* 26 (Spring 1965), 30-37

Kennedy, Ruby Jo Reeves, "Premarital Residential Propinquity and Ethnic Endogamy," *American Journal of Sociology* 48 (March 1943), 580-584

———, "Single or Triple Melting-Pot? Intermarriage Trends in New Haven, 1870-1940," *American Journal of Sociology* 49 (January 1944), 331-339

———, "Single or Triple Melting-Pot? Intermarriage Trends in New Haven, 1870-1950," *American Journal of Sociology* 58 (July 1952), 56-59

Kiser, Clyde V., "Assortative Mating by Educational Attainment in Relation to Fertility," *Eugenics Quarterly* 15 (June 1968), 98-112

Knoke, David, "A Comparison of Log-Linear and Regression Models for Systems of Dichotomous Variables," *Sociological Methods and Research* 3 (May 1975), 416-434

Kolemainen, John I., "The Finns of Wisconsin," *Wisconsin Magazine of History* 27 (June 1944), 391-399

Koller, Marvin R., "Residential Propinquity of White Mates at Marriage in Relation to Age and Occupation of Males, Columbus, Ohio, 1938 and 1946," *American Sociological Review* 13 (October 1948), 613-616

Kouser, J. Morgan, "Ecological Regression and the Analysis of Past Politics," *Journal of Interdisciplinary History* 4 (Autumn 1973), 237-262

———, "The 'New Political History:' A Methodological Critique," *Reviews in American History* 4 (March 1976), 1-14

Krontoft, Torben, "Factors in Assimilation: A Comparative Study," *Norwegian-American Studies* 26 (1974), 184-205

Kuzniewski, Anthony J., "Milwaukee Poles, 1866-1918: The Rise and Fall of a Model Community," *Milwaukee History* 1 (Spring-Summer 1978), 13-24

Landis, Paul H., and Day, Katherine H., "Education as a Factor in Mate Selection," *American Sociological Review* 10 (August 1945), 558-560

Levi, Kate A. Everest, "Early Lutheran Immigration to Wisconsin," *Transactions of the Wisconsin Academy of Sciences, Arts, and Letters* 8 (1892), 289-298

———, "Geographical Origins of German Immigration to Wisconsin," *Collections of the State Historical Society of Wisconsin* 14 (1898), 341-393

———, "How Wisconsin Came By Its Large German Element," *Collections of the State Historical Society of Wisconsin* 12 (1892), 299-334

Lichtman, Allan J., "Correlation, Regression, and the Ecological Fallacy," *Journal of Interdisciplinary History* 3 (Winter 1974), 417-433

Lieberson, Stanley, "The Price-Zubrzycki Measure of Ethnic Intermarriage," *Eugenics Quarterly* 13 (March 1966), 92-100

Locke, Harvey J., Sabagh, G., and Thomes, M. M., "Interfaith Marriages," *Social Problems* 4 (April 1957), 329-333

Lucas, Henry S., "The First Dutch Settlers in Milwaukee," *Wisconsin Magazine of History* 30 (December 1946), 174-183

———, "The Founding of New Amsterdam in La Crosse County," *Wisconsin Magazine of History* 31 (September 1947), 42-60

Luchsinger, John, "The Planting of the Swiss Colony at New Glarus," *Collections of the State Historical Society of Wisconsin* 12 (1892), 335-382

———, "The Swiss Colony of New Glarus," *Collections of the State Historical Society of Wisconsin* 8 (1879), 411-439

Malin, James C., "The Turnover of Farm Population in Kansas," *Kansas Historical Quarterly* 4 (November 1935), 339-372

Marches, Joseph R., and Turbeville, Gus, "The Effect of Residential Propinquity on Marriage Selection," *American Journal of Sociology* 58 (May 1953), 592-595

Marcson, Simon, "A Theory of Intermarriage and Assimilation," *Social Forces* 29 (October 1950), 75-78

Martin, Xavier, "Belgians of Northeastern Wisconsin," *Proceedings of the State Historical Society of Wisconsin* 13 (1895), 375-396

Marvin, Donald M., "Occupational Propinquity as a Factor in Marriage Selection," *Quarterly Publications of the American Statistical Association* 16 (September 1918), 131-150

Mashek, Nan, "Bohemian Farmers in Wisconsin," *Charities* 13 (December 1904), 211-214

McClusky, Howard Y., and Zander, Alvin, "Residential Propinquity and Marriage in Branch County, Michigan," *Social Forces* 19 (October 1940), 79-81

McKain, Walter C., Jr., and Anderson, C. Arnold, "Assortative Mating in Prosperity and Depression," *Sociology and Social Research* 21 (May-June 1937), 411-418

Meloni, Alberto C., "Italy Invades the Bloody Third: The Early History of Milwaukee's Italians," *Historical Messenger* 25 (March 1969), 34-45

Merton, Robert K., "Intermarriage and the Social Structure: Fact and Theory," *Psychiatry* 4 (August 1941), 361-374

Metzner, Lee, "The Belgians in the North Country," *Wisconsin Magazine of History* 26 (March 1943), 280-288

Mittelbach, Frank G., and Moore, Joan W., "Ethnic Endogamy—The Case of Mexican-Americans," *American Journal of Sociology* 74 (July 1968), 50-62

Munch, Peter A., "Segregation and Assimilation of Norwegian Settlements in Wisconsin," *Norwegian-American Studies and Records* 18 (1954), 102-140

Murguia, Edward, and Frisbie, W. Parker, "Trends in Mexican American Intermarriage: Recent Findings in Perspective," *Social Science Quarterly* 58 (December 1977), 374-389

Murstein, Bernard I., "Stimulus—Value—Role: A Theory of Marital Choice," *Journal of Marriage and the Family* 32 (August 1970), 465-481

Nelson, Lowry, "Intermarriage Among Nationality Groups in a Rural Area of Minnesota," *American Journal of Sociology* 48 (March 1943), 585-592

Panunzio, Constantine, "Intermarriage in Los Angeles, 1924-1933," *American Journal of Sociology* 47 (March 1942), 690-701

Parkman, Margaret A., and Sawyer, Jack, "Dimensions of Intermarriage in Hawaii," *American Sociological Review* 32 (August 1967), 593-607

Perry, P. J., "Working-Class Isolation and Mobility in Rural Dorset, 1837-1936: A Study of Marriage Distances," *Transactions of the Institute of British Geographers,* No. 46 (March 1969), 121-141

Pienkos, Donald, "Politics, Religion and Change in Polish Milwaukee, 1900-1930," *Wisconsin Magazine of History* 61 (Spring 1976), 179-209

Price, C. A., and Zubrzycki, J., "The Use of Inter-Marriage Statistics as an Index of Assimilation," *Population Studies* 16 (July 1962), 58-69

Price, Sadie Rowlands, "The Welsh of Waukesha County," *Wisconsin Magazine of History* 26 (March 1943), 323-332

Prisland, Marie, "The Slovenians, Most Recent American Immigrants," *Wisconsin Magazine of History* 33 (March 1950), 265-280

Resnik, Reuben B., "Some Sociological Aspects of Intermarriage of Jew and Non-Jew," *Social Forces* 12 (October 1933), 94-102

Richardson, Helen M., "Studies of Mental Resemblance Between Husband and Wives and Between Friends," *Psychological Bulletin* 36 (January 1939), 104-120

Risdon, Randal, "A Study of Interracial Marriages Based on Data for Los Angeles County," *Sociology and Social Research* 39 (November-December 1954), 92-95

Rodman, Hyman, "Technical Note on Two Rates of Mixed Marriage," *American Sociological Review* 30 (October 1965), 776-778

Rosen, Lawrence, and Bell, Robert R., "Mate Selection in the Upper Class," *Sociological Quarterly* 7 (Spring 1966), 157-166

Saloutos, Theodore, "The Greeks in Milwaukee," *Wisconsin Magazine of History* 53 (Spring 1970), 175-193

Schafer, Joseph, "The Yankee and the Teuton in Wisconsin," series in the *Wisconsin Magazine of History* 6:125-279, 386-402 and 6:148-171

Schmitt, Robert C., Demographic Correlates of Interracial Marriage in Hawaii," *Demography* 2 (1965), 463-473

——, "Recent Trends of Hawaiian Interracial Marriage Rates by Occupation," *Journal of Marriage and the Family* 33 (May 1971), 373-374

Schoen, Robert *et al,* "Intermarriage Among Spanish Surnamed Californians, 1962-1974," *International Migration Review* 12 (Fall 1978), 359-369

Schultz, Gwen, "Evolution of the Areal Patterns of German and Polish Settlement in Milwaukee," *Erdkunde* 10 (1956), 136-140

Semmingsen, Ingrid Gaustad, "Norwegian Emigration to America During the Nineteenth Century," *Norwegian-American Studies and Records* 11 (1940), 66-81

Simon, Roger D., "Housing and Services in an Immigrant Neighborhood," *Journal of Urban History* 2 (August 1976), 435-458

Sindberg, R. M., Roberts, A. F. and McClain, D., "Mate Selection Factors in Computer Matched Marriages," *Journal of Marriage and the Family* 34 (November 1972), 611-614

Slotkin, J. S., "Jewish-Gentile Intermarriage in Chicago," *American Sociological Review* 7 (February 1942), 34-39

Smith, Guy-Harold, "Notes on the Distribution of the Foreign-Born Scandinavians in Wisconsin in 1905," *Wisconsin Magazine of History* 14 (June 1931), 419-436

——, "Notes on the Distribution of the German-Born in Wisconsin," *Wisconsin Magazine of History* 13 (December 1929), 107-120

——, "The Populating of Wisconsin," *Geographical Review* 18 (July 1928), 402-421

——, "Settlement and Distribution of the Population in Wisconsin," *Transactions of the Wisconsin Academy of Sciences, Arts, and Letters* 24 (1929), 53-107

Spuhler, J. N., "Assortative Mating with Respect to the Physical Characteristics," *Eugenics Quarterly* 15 (June 1968), 128-139

Stouffer, Samuel A., "Intervening Opportunities: A Theory Relating Mobility and Distance," *American Sociological Review* 5 (December 1940), 845-867

Sundal, A. Philip, and McCormick, Thomas C., "Age at Marriage and Mate Selection: Madison, Wisconsin, 1937-1943," *American Sociological Review* 16 (February 1951), 37-48

Thomas, John E., "Pioneer Settlement of Sheboygan County," *Collections of the State Historical Society of Wisconsin* 9 (1880-82), 389-396

Thomas, John L., "The Factor of Religion in the Selection of Marriage Mates," *American Sociological Review* 16 (August 1951), 487-491

Tomkiewicz, John W. S., "Polanders in Wisconsin," *Proceedings of the State Historical Society of Wisconsin, 1901* (1901), 148-152

Traynor, Victor J., "Urban and Rural Mixed Marriage," *Social Order* 6 (April 1956), 154-162

Trost, Jan, "Some Data on Mate Selection, Homogamy and Perceived Homogamy," *Journal of Marriage and the Family* 29 (November 1967), 739-755

Udry, J. Richard, "The Influence of the Ideal Mate Image on Mate Selection and Mate Perception," *Journal of Marriage and the Family* 27 (November 1965), 477-482

_____, Bauman, Karl E., and Chase, Charles, "Skin Color, Status, and Mate Selection," *American Journal of Sociology* 76 (January 1971), 722-733

Usher, Ellis B., "New England Influence in Milwaukee," *Proceedings of the State Historical Society, 1901* (1901), 170-174

Vlach, J. J., "Our Bohemian Population," *Proceedings of the State Historical Society of Wisconsin, 1901* (1901), 159-162

Warren, Bruce L., "A Multiple Variable Approach to the Assortative Mating Phenomenon," *Eugenics Quarterly* 13 (December 1966), 285-290

Weatherly, Ulysses G., "Race and Marriage," *American Journal of Sociology* 15 (January 1910), 433-453

White, Harry K., "The Icelanders in Washington Island," *Collections of the State Historical Society of Wisconsin* 54 (1898), 335-340

Willits, Fern K., Bealer, Robert C., and Bender, Gerald W., "Interreligious Marriage Among Pennsylvania Rural Youth," *Marriage and Family Living* 25 (November 1963), 433-438

Winch, Robert F., "Another Look at the Theory of Complementary Needs in Mate Selection," *Journal of Marriage and the Family* 29 (November 1967), 756-762

Yinger, J. Milton, and Simpson, George Eater, "The Integration of Americans of Indian Descent," *Annals of the American Academy of Political and Social Science* 436 (March 1978), 137-151

Zick, Rubin, "Do American Women Marry Up?" *American Sociological Review* 33 (October 1968), 750-760

Zipf, George K., " 'The P_1P_2/D' Hypothesis: On the Intercity Movement of Persons," *American Sociological Review* 11 (December 1946), 677-686

Dissertations and Theses

Alba, R. D., "Assimilation Among American Catholics," Ph.D., Columbia University, 1974

Bremer, Richard G., "Furrows Along the Loup: The Social and Economic History of a Great Plains Farming Region, 1910-1970," Ph.D., University of Wisconsin, Madison, 1973

Brown, Mona, "The Jewish Community in Racine, Wisconsin: A Study in Human Eco-logy," M.A., Marquette University, 1942

Cohen, Steven M., "Patterns of Ethnic Marriage and Friendship in the United States," Ph.D., Columbia University, 1974

Fonkalsrud, Alfred O., "Scandinavians as a Social Force in America," Ph.D., New York University, 1913

Galford, Justin B., "The Foreign Born and Urban Growth in the Great Lakes, 1850-1950: A Study of Chicago, Cleveland, Detroit and Milwaukee," Ph.D., New York University, 1957

Kimmerle, Marjorie M., "Norwegian Surnames of the Koshkonong and Springdale Con-gregations in Dane County, Wisconsin," Ph.D., University of Wisconsin, Madison, 1938

Lang, Edward M., Jr., "The Common Man in Janesville, Wisconsin, 1870-1900, M.A., University of Wisconsin, Madison, 1968

Laugesen, Peter N., "The Immigrants of Madison, Wisconsin, 1860-1890," M.A. Uni-versity of Wisconsin, Madison, 1966

Litzow, Joseph A., "Poles in Milwaukee, 1906-1909," M.A., St. Francis Seminary, 1944

Pedersen, Harald A., "Acculturation Among Danish and Polish Ethnic Groups in Wis-consin," Ph.D., University of Wisconsin, Madison, 1949

Reeves, Ruby Jo, "Marriages in New Haven Since 1870, Statistically Analyzed and Cul-turally Interpreted," Ph.D., Yale University, 1938

Stampen, Jacob Ola, "The Norwegian Element of Madison, Wisconsin, 1850-1900: A Study in Ethnic Assimilation," M.A., University of Wisconsin, Madison, 1965

Strub, Paul E., "The Rise of Industrial Manitowoc, Wisconsin," B.A., University of Wisconsin, Madison, 1931

Sutherland, Laura, "The Immigrant Family in the City' Milwaukee's Poles, 1880-1905," M.A., University of Wisconsin-Milwaukee, 1974

Tagliavia, Salvatore J., "Italians in Milwaukee," M.A., St. Francis Seminary, 1946

Travis, Harry Paul, "Religious In-Marriage and Inter-Marriage in Canada, 1934-1969: A Methodological and Empirical Investigation," M.S., University of Wisconsin, Madi-son, 1973

Other

Ankarloo, Bengt, "Marriage," unpublished paper presented to the MSSB Conference, Williams College, July 20-28, 1975, photocopied

Richard, Madeline A., and Campbell, Douglas F., "The Differential Effects of Religion and the Cultural Setting on Ethnic Intermarriage in Toronto and Montreal, 1971," unpublished paper presented at the Population Association of America Meeting, Atlanta, Georgia, 1978

Roeseler, John S., papers, 1 box, State Historical Society of Wisconsin, Madison

"Wisconsin State Census—Studies for 1905," unpublished study originally entitled: "Ethnic Backgrounds in Wisconsin," under the direction of George Hill, Department of Rural Sociology, University of Wisconsin, 1937-40, State Historical Society of Wisconsin, Madison

Index

Index